risk
IN OUR MIDST

Empowering Teenagers to Love the Unlovable

by scott larson

with contributions from dr. john hoover

Group

Loveland, Colorado

acknowledgments

Thanks to Dell Erwin, John Kinsley, and Mike Laurence for their invaluable input and insights. Thanks also to Jim Kochenburger at Group Publishing for encouraging me to keep forging ahead, especially during those times when it just didn't seem to be coming together. Most of all, thanks to John Hoover, who knows the topic of bullying perhaps better than anyone and brought all of that research together with his faith to help make this book something of real substance. Our prayers are that it will make a difference in the lives of those kids who need it most.

risk IN OUR MIDST

Copyright © 2000 Scott Larson

Visit our Web site: **www.grouppublishing.com**

CREDITS

Contributing Writer: Dr. John Hoover
Editor: Michael D. Warden
Creative Development Editor: Jim Kochenburger
Chief Creative Officer: Joani Schultz
Copy Editor: Lyndsay E. Bierce
Designer: Jean Bruns
Computer Graphic Artist: Anita M. Cook
Cover Art Director: Jeff A. Storm
Cover Designer: Coonts Design Group, LLC
Cover Illustrator: Mary GrandPre
Production Manager: Dodie Tipton

ISBN 0-7644-2248-0

10 9 8 7 6 5 4 3 2 1   09 08 07 06 05 04 03 02 01 00

Printed in the United States of America.

contents

about the authors

THE REV. SCOTT LARSON, D.MIN., is president of Straight Ahead Ministries, which he co-founded with his wife, Hanne. Straight Ahead operates Bible studies in more than one hundred fifty juvenile detention centers in twelve states. They also provide aftercare mentoring programs and discipleship homes. Dr. Larson has written three additional books: *At Risk: Bringing Hope to Hurting Teenagers* for youth workers; *Reclaiming Our Prodigal Sons and Daughters* for teachers and social workers; and *A Way Out* for youth. He also designed an assessment tool for youth called *Quick Connect*. The Larsons are parents of two children and reside in Northborough, Massachusetts.

JOHN HOOVER, PH.D., is professor of special education at the University of North Dakota, Grand Forks as well as director of the Bureau of Educational Services and Applied Research. Dr. Hoover is a leading researcher on the topic of bullying. He has co-authored a curriculum for public schools called the *Bullying Prevention Handbook*, and *Teasing and Harassment: A Guide for Parents and Teachers* as well as numerous research articles on bullying. Dr. Hoover and his wife Betsy are active members of St. Paul's Episcopal Church. They have three children.

Note: *All the stories in this book are true, but some of the names of young people have been changed. Names of adults have not been changed. Illustrations are written in the first person as Scott Larson unless otherwise indicated.*

foreword

RICH VAN PELT

Several years ago I met with the administrator of a Christian school system after he had just completed an interview with a couple interested in transferring their children to his school. Academic standards were important and the school's extracurricular activities were appealing, but this mom and dad were really only interested in his answer to the one big question they posed: "If our kids attend your school, will they be exposed to drinking and drugs, sex, violence, and those sorts of things." He thought for a bit and responded, "We're a school in the reformed tradition—*we're not a reform school.*"

At the time I was serving as chaplain at one of Colorado's lock-up facilities for adolescent offenders. Our staff had to contend regularly with kids verbally and physically abusing each other, using illicit drugs, and acting out sexually. Even in *reform school* we were incapable of the kind of control that this couple was seeking in a *private school* environment. From their perspective, the parents were simply looking for a place where their children would be safe.

The events of the past few years have taught us that there really is no such place—a place where our kids can feel "safe" and we can be totally assured of their welfare. Children and adolescents have been gunned down in school classrooms, libraries, cafeterias, playgrounds, and even during youth rallies at church. While concern for their children's physical safety is at an all-time high, parents and youth workers must be equally concerned for the children's emotional safety.

Few would argue that it has never been more challenging to raise kids or to be one. The ravages of battle are everywhere to be seen.

James Garbarino is professor of human development at Cornell University and author of *Lost Boys: Why Our Sons Turn Violent and How We Can Save Them*. Writing in the December 20, 1999 issue of Time magazine, Garbarino comments, "The normal culture of adolescence today contains elements that are so nasty that it becomes hard for parents (and professionals) to distinguish between what in a teenager's talk, dress and taste in music, films and video games indicates psychological trouble and what is simply a sign of the times. Most kids who subscribe to the trench-coated Goth lifestyle, or have multiple body piercings, or listen to Marilyn Manson, or play the video game Doom are normal kids caught in a toxic culture."[1]

By definition, a "toxic" culture is ultimately destructive—poisonous. In a matter of time the toxins gain control and, in the absence of an antidote, sickness and death soon follow. The toxins in our culture are at work and, not surprisingly, they are most effective in the lives of those most vulnerable.

Risk in Our Midst is one "antidote" worth your serious attention. Scott Larson is a nationally recognized youth ministry specialist providing direction for Straight Ahead Ministries and its outreach to juvenile offenders. I have grown to respect the depth of Scott's heart for kids traditionally forgotten, intentionally ignored, or purposely alienated by mainstream youth ministry programs. I am encouraged by his determination to call the church of Jesus to sacrificially care for the "least of these."

But who are the least of these? We might be surprised.

How many youth groups spend thousands of dollars to travel thousands of miles to reach out to people groups who are already being reached by those who live among them? Very little of eternal significance is accomplished by many of these trips, but we leave feeling good about ourselves and pumped for the next opportunity to go to the far reaches of the earth with the "good news of the gospel."

Unfortunately, nothing has changed when the school bell rings on Monday morning and our young "saints" walk the halls and attend classes at East High. Not unlike their pagan friends, kids from our youth group ignore the cries of loneliness, alienation, despair, and fear that scream from the desks nearby. What's more, they resent the bullies (because many are victims themselves) but would never risk defending those bullied for fear of being too closely identified with them.

In a day when many parents are frantically seeking places where kids can be safe, Scott Larson is calling a generation of committed Christian youth workers and students to move out of their comfort zones and literally *become* a place of safety for those in need. His message is anything but sentimentalized Christianity and bubble gum youth ministry.

Psalm 62:7-8 reads, "My help and glory are in God—granite-strength and safe-harbor-God—So trust him absolutely, people; lay your lives on the line for him. God is a safe place to be" (*The Message*).

The promise is true. He is safe but he calls his people to anything but a safe lifestyle. One of my friends likes to say that Jesus promises peace, power, purpose, and trouble! Taking up your cross daily means more than wearing a piece of jewelry.

Essentially, Jesus said "come and die to yourself." We do kids a serious disservice when we call them to anything but a biblical Christianity. It's easy to identify the toxins in the culture. But what of those in the church?

Jim Hancock is a veteran youth worker and a really bright guy. In his book *Raising Adults: Getting Kids Ready for the Real World*, Jim reminds parents of the power of their example: "Toxicity is not out there. It's an inside job. And in the parts that *are* influenced by outside forces, our kids listen to and learn from us first, before their peers. In many ways, they follow our examples to excruciating lengths. Only the details of their behavior are different."[2]

It has been said that you can take kids only as far along as you've gone yourself. Is it equally true that you will take kids only as far as you are willing to go yourself? Author Tim Hansel is fond of saying that "we've never learned to plug our theology into our biography"[3] Perhaps that's our problem. We don't really believe that Jesus loves everyone. We give the notion intellectual assent but our faith doesn't really influence the way we treat the convenience store clerk, the toll collector, or the bagger at the grocery store. What we are speaks so loudly that kids can't hear what we say.

This generation is begging for authenticity.

Risk in Our Midst is the most convicting and empowering youth ministry book I have read in years. It will challenge and equip you to challenge and equip your kids to take a giant step of faith and reach out to the outcasts in their midst.

risk
IN OUR MIDST

kids
on the
fringe

trouble
unforeseen

No one would argue that Brian was a difficult child for other classmates to like. For one thing, he was overweight—an attribute that youngsters find difficult to accept in a peer. He also suffered from attention-deficit disorder. And though he displayed a lively sense of humor, Brian was also prone to interrupt conversations and become overexcited, often causing embarrassment to those around him. Yet he had such a tender heart. His mother described him as possessing "a keen sense of right and wrong," often feeling "frustrated by the cruelty and injustice he saw in the world."

Brian grew up in a loving family, but they had no idea how much he internalized the laughter and snickers of others. He just didn't talk about it. Instead, he seemed to extend forgiveness and freely grant the benefit of the doubt. Most of Brian's classmates didn't think much about it either. In the world of middle school madness, Brian didn't take up much space. A quiet, pudgy kid, he was sort of *out of sight, out of mind.*

That's why everyone was so shocked the day this fourteen-year-old came to school carrying a concealed weapon and, in the school cafeteria, ended his life by shooting himself. Perhaps he chose the cafeteria because it had come to symbolize so much of the torture he endured.

Days later, when his parents found some of his poetry, they began to understand the depth of pain Brian had internalized from years of relentless teasing, torment, and verbal abuse from peers. His writings speak for thousands:

> *For all my life I have lived with the words that haunt me. The words of*
> *America's sadistic children. Children who had been so distorted by*
> *the images of insult to all those who are "different" that they don't*
> *even have the capability to understand that what they do is wrong.*

Although the light is wide in its spread,
   they still cannot see the pain on my face.
The pain that their eyes bring to bear when they look upon me.
They see me as an insignificant "thing," something to be traded,
   mangled and mocked.

You may search for us all your days, but never find us.
We are everywhere, yet we are nowhere.[1]

Does the church have a message for kids like Brian? Might an embracing youth group have made a difference in his life? Sadly, he had never been invited to such a function. Might the story have ended differently if he had been? We will never know. Only one thing is for sure: Our schools and communities are filled with thousands more like Brian.

BULLYING

For some, the teenage years are marked with fond memories of friends, romances, school dances, malls, and amusement parks. But for others it is more like a never-ending nightmare. Called cruel names and being the butt of jokes, they sit alone in school cafeterias, are labeled and lied about, are shoved into school lockers, and are even beaten on an almost-daily basis.

When adults hear the term "bullying," many envision an imposing boy on an elementary school playground picking on a smaller child. While it does encompass that, bullying, as we are describing it, goes much broader and deeper. We would define it as "the repeated negative acts by one or more youngsters against another." Such negative acts could be verbal or physical in nature, such as hitting, kicking, teasing, or taunting. Or they might be indirect, as in manipulating friendships or purposely excluding others from activities. Implicit in this definition is the imbalance of real or perceived power between bully and victim, making the bully's intimidating threats a legitimate fear.[2]

Tragically, bullying has reached near epidemic proportion in the United States. Seventy-five percent of today's youngsters report being bullied by peers, with 90 percent admitting to side effects such as a drop in grades, increased anxiety, or a loss of friends or social life.[3] Fifteen percent of victims have been severely traumatized.[4] While some adults might downplay its severity with the notion that "kids will be kids," it is unlikely that these same grown-ups would tolerate such taunting and physical harassment in their own lives.

Though bullying occurs at a rate four times higher in the United States than in places like Great Britain, other countries have taken it much more seriously.[5] For example, England has actually launched an Anti-Bullying Campaign similar in scope to our own anti-drug and anti-violence campaigns. Its purpose is to help kids who are either bullying or being bullied, and their hot line receives more than sixteen thousand calls a year.[6]

Tragically, one of the common denominators running through the unfortunate stories of school violence in the past several years is this reality: Each perpetrator was brutally picked on by peers.[7]

DERRICK

"Dorky Derrick, the Walking Encyclopedia!" These words were a sure indication that yet another prank was about to be played. More knees would be skinned. More dignity—that precious and rare commodity for an eighth-grader—deducted from the already meager store. "Dorky Derrick! Dorky Derrick!" The call was clear each morning on the school bus. It rang out at lunch when teachers' backs were turned, and sometimes when they were not. It continued on the way home from school, accompanied by having his books dumped and being shoved into mud puddles or snow banks.

An intelligent boy, Derrick often wondered what pleasure it gave classmates to ridicule him. In past years, he had lost his temper and had even been in a fight or two over the name-calling. But the bigger boys had made two things indelibly clear. First, he was going to be Dorky Derrick forever, whether he liked it or not. Second, any student who wanted to could call him that, for the more aggressive boys would protect the few who were less physically able than Derrick.

Derrick had learned to put forth a convincing but false face of equanimity.

Until the day he borrowed his father's 9 mm pistol and took it to school in a book bag. He must have thought about the gun all morning. Just after lunch, as students were settling into their fifth-hour English class, the call "Dorky Derrick" started up. Derrick reached into the book bag and drew out the pistol. Two of the boys who had been taunting him for years died within seconds of one another. Seeming to emerge from a dream, Derrick looked at the carnage, put the gun to his own head, and pulled the trigger.

Unlike Brian, Derrick had actually attended several Christian youth groups. But not seeing a marked difference between church and the environment he had experienced in school, the effect on him was relatively insignificant. Perhaps it was because he was at the bottom of the schoolyard ladder. Shy and overweight, Derrick wasn't the sort of kid you build a thriving program around. But as Christians, what is our responsibility to such kids?

WHERE ARE WE HEADED?

In the weeks and months following the tragedy, shock and disbelief paralyzed the entire community. Derrick was such a nice kid. He certainly didn't fit the profile of a killer or even a "troubled youth." From a two-parent family in a middle-class suburb, he was talented, intelligent, and had a great future ahead of him.

People everywhere are perplexed about how kids like Derrick can be driven to the edge, committing some of the most heinous crimes in recent history. While school hate crimes are always wrong and inexcusable, it is not difficult to see how young people are brought to such destructive paths. Children who suffer the brunt of merciless and sustained bullying can eventually come to a place where they feel that they can take no more.

Fear and anxiety have a way of erupting into volcanic rage over time, causing some to lash back and even the score in a final act of vengeance. As a result of Paducah, Jonesboro, and Littleton, desperate and hopeless children who were already contemplating suicide now saw how they could take out some of the people who had caused them such pain before ending their own lives.

Enraged kids have found Eric Harris and Dylan Klebold of Littleton, Colorado, to be a long-awaited mouthpiece for their own buried feelings. In the month following the Littleton massacre in 1999, more than four hundred copycat threats were made. This dramatic response demonstrates how one tragic act of retribution had deeply resonated with countless young people whose own fury was bottled up inside.

For example, shortly after the shooting, one young man wrote an essay on his own experience of being bullied and placed it on his personal Web site. He said, "I know exactly how these guys feel. I have my own list of people I'd kill if I had the guts." Within three days he had received more than six thousand "hits" from other students who had found his site and could relate to how he felt.[8]

A week after the Columbine High School shootings, one North Dakota student expressed similar feelings in a "Letter to the Editor" of his college newspaper:

"Between grades seven and nine, I was one of those kids that everyone picked on. I was an easy target, I had few friends and for three years, I absolutely dreaded the seven hours a day that I had to be in school. The work itself was no problem. I had nearly a 4.0, but as I'm sure everyone knows, kids that age are extremely cruel to those who are too shy and insecure to fight back. For those three years, I endured almost constant heckling, book dumpings and I was hit on numerous occasions. In that time, not a single adult teacher stepped up for me.

"I can vividly remember many walks to school each morning trying to concoct a plan to either kill myself or those [jerks] who never let me be. The only thing that ever stopped me was that I could not work up the guts to actually do it.

"[I'm twenty-two years old now, but] I have no doubt at all that what happened in Colorado last week would have happened here in Grand Forks by my hand. It's only a matter of time before some fifteen-year-old comes along who has the guts to use a gun to take care of problems that the teachers and other faculty members had been completely oblivious to."[9]

BRIGHT SPOTS

At the very time our schools are becoming more dangerous and perplexing, God is moving in unprecedented ways in the lives of Christian teens. In two decades of youth ministry I have not witnessed such a profound move of the Holy Spirit. Everywhere I go, I hear of kids wanting to trade in games and fun activities for more intense worship, a deeper sense of community, and outward acts of service. A leader from one large church recently told me of her experience. Four years ago, this church had over twelve hundred high school students at its weekly outreach events and two hundred attending its more intense discipleship nights. Now they average about six hundred at each. One thing is for sure: This generation of young people wants to go deeper.

Perhaps it is not coincidental that the very point at which record numbers of kids are being ostracized and victimized, Christian young people are desiring to be more radically used by God. Perhaps the kids who need our youth groups most do not reside on the other side of the world. Many of them live right next door. The world they know, however, is a million miles away from the one experienced by most of the kids in our youth groups. But biblically functioning youth groups may be in a position to do more than anything else in our culture to avert tragedies like those we have seen in the past few years. Such groups may be the means God uses to bring authentic healing to so many battered and outcast children.

Why does such healing happen so infrequently? No doubt, there are multiple barriers to overcome: Barriers within ourselves and our kids who jump at the chance to travel across the world, but reel at the prospect of filling our youth groups with outcasts and nerds; barriers in the culture of our churches that resist embracing those they see as being vastly different from themselves; barriers from bullied kids themselves who have come to distrust churches and the people who fill them.

This book is about trying to understand and deal with those barriers. It is a worthwhile endeavor since doing so could well unleash the greatest revival in the history of youth culture. Any true movement of God in our young people could not exclude kids like Brian and Derrick. In fact, history would testify to the notion that such kids might just be leading it, for God has always chosen the "weak things of this world to put the powerful to shame" (1 Corinthians 1:27, The Contemporary English Version).

who is my neighbor?

Of the thousands of youth and adults who encountered Brian and Derrick, most didn't tease, torment, or ridicule them. In fact, only a handful made these boys' lives so unbearable. But what about all those who didn't actively participate? The ones who may have shaken their heads in disapproval, but then turned and walked the other way? Those who didn't want to get involved? The ones afraid of what others might think? What responsibility do they bear?

A PARABLE FOR OUR TIMES

Jesus was confronted by a young, self-righteous lawyer in Luke 10:25-37. Wanting to test Jesus, he asked, "What must I do to inherit eternal life?"

When Jesus turned the question back on him, he proudly quoted from the books of Deuteronomy and Leviticus, " 'Love the Lord your God with all your heart and with all your soul and with all your strength and with all your mind'; and, 'Love your neighbor as yourself.' "

"You have answered correctly," Jesus assured him. "Do this and you will live."

Not wanting to let Jesus off the hook quite so easily, the young attorney continued his interrogation, "And who is my neighbor?"

The text indicates that the young man was at least partially motivated by a need to justify himself. Certainly, as an upstanding member of the Jewish community, he had mastered the art of "good neighboring." After having suffered under Roman rule for nearly a century, known oppression by the Greeks for 270 years before that, only to be preceded by 250 years of Babylonian and Persian dictatorships, the Jewish people had learned well how to care for one another. But when Jesus, by inference, defined a good neighbor as a *Samaritan*—those no-good, half-breeds that Jews despised— that was a bit more than he could stomach.

WHO IS MY NEIGHBOR?

One of the problems with reading a first century parable with twenty-first century lenses is the natural disconnection to customs, characters, and culture. Perhaps a contemporary paraphrase of the parable might look something like this:

Frank came to dread school more and more as the semester dragged on, especially that torturous hallway he was forced to travel three days a week on his way to third-period math class. The turf was ruled by upper-class jocks whose behavior was predictable.

"Hey, it's 'Four-Eyes Frankie!' " they would shout as he rounded the corner. Frank would walk faster to hasten the torture's end and minimize the humiliation. The scene was all too familiar. Four or five letter-jacketed boys quickly assumed a defensive lineman posture, blocking the entire hallway. Someone on the sidelines would yell, "Hut, hut!" while others chanted, "Go Frankie, go!"

The more Frank tried to hurry through with minimum scathing, the more laughter and jeers rang out. Inevitably, Frank would be tackled, either immediately or fifteen feet later as boys twice his size let him squeeze through the line only to chase him down as they made ape-like sounds. As Frank lay sprawled out on the floor amidst books, calculator, and glasses, on-lookers cheered, "First down!" or "Roughing the quarterback!"

Then the bell would ring, and fellow students would chuckle as they funneled into classrooms. Frank would enter class a couple minutes late as he tried to bring order to his disheveled papers before entering.

Teachers knew the routine as well as the students. They would hear the commotion outside their classrooms, but were too busy writing outlines on chalkboards or with other last minute details to risk the potential fallout of confronting such a seemingly "harmless tradition."

No doubt some of the Christian students had also observed how this wasn't very "Christlike" behavior. But to confront the so-called leaders of their school would even further ostracize them from the mainstream. They were concentrating on making inroads into this group in order to better reach them. Making a scene about something like this would only further alienate them.

And so the ritual continued unopposed. That is until Ron finally stood up. "Why don't you jerks pick on someone your own size?" That brought the house down as Ron was a member of the high school's Gay and Lesbian Society.

While Frank's days of being picked on didn't end there, friendship and support was extended to him for the first time that year.

Now, which of these do you think was a good neighbor?

If you find yourself angered and offended by such a rendition, congratulations—you got the point! That is exactly the response Jesus engendered when he told it.

This parable is applicable to each of us who encounter kids like Frank every day. It speaks to our youth group members as well because they meet such kids far more frequently than we do and are in an even better position to do something about it.

The first similarity between the first-century parable and the more contemporary one lies in their overall contexts. Many listening to Jesus' parable might well have concluded, "Hey, anyone traveling down that road alone *needs* to be taught a lesson. If he's that stupid he deserves to be robbed and beaten up."

The eighteen-mile stretch from Jerusalem to Jericho wasn't nicknamed "The Bloody Way" for nothing. The narrow, rocky defiles, sudden turnings, and thirty-six-hundred-foot drop in elevation made it a happy hunting ground for bandits and thieves.[1] This traveler was obviously a reckless and foolhardy character to attempt this road, especially while carrying valuable items. He had no one to blame but himself for his plight.

Likewise, studies reveal that the vast majority of today's middle and high school students believe that victims of bullying actually bring it on themselves, that somehow they have it coming. The same majority agrees that bullying can actually be useful in helping those students by making them tougher. In fact, nearly half of American teens believe that bullying is at least partially "instructive" in that it teaches the victim about behavior that is unacceptable to the group.[2]

The second similarity involves the inconvenience that an encounter with such a victim inevitably produces. In Jesus' story, the priest and the Levite were obviously busy people. No doubt, they were on their way to some important function and didn't have time to stop. Add to that the potential risk of being attacked if one stopped for a prolonged period of time on such a dangerous stretch and it is not surprising that they kept moving.

The priest faced an additional risk as well. Uncertain whether or not this stranger was dead, he knew the command of Numbers 19:11. It declared that anyone who touched a dead body would be considered unclean for seven days. For the priest, stopping could mean a forfeiture of his turn of duty at the temple. In the end, he chose the claims of ceremonial service above those of charity.

Kids who consider reaching out to bullied peers face their own set of risks as well. Going out of the way to touch the lives of those lying on the side of the road is not very enticing. Just as in the parable, maimed kids require more than a mere nod of good gesture. Their needs can be very consuming.

Beyond just the commitment of time and energy, half of today's students acknowledge that befriending a scapegoat would likely result in reducing their own social standing among peers,[3] not to mention the potential risk of being picked on themselves. Not surprisingly, most of us would prefer to stand by rather than risk the safety we currently enjoy.

The third similarity involves the perceived responsibility of bystanders Most of us might suffer a twinge of guilt if we were part of the band of perpetrators who picked on innocent kids. Just the fact that we *don't* participate in such activities gives us some sense of pride, knowing we're not as bad as those other guys. But Jesus didn't leave such a convenient option—not to the lawyer in first-century Palestine, and not to us. He defined *loving our neighbor* much more broadly than simply *not* participating in the direct abuse of others. He clearly taught that standing by silently observing such antics was just as bad as participating directly in them.

Fourth, and possibly the most significant, is who the Samaritans represented in Jesus' day. They were half-breeds who didn't fit into the homogeneous Jewish culture. Detestable to most Jews, Samaritans were regularly referred to as "dogs." Likewise, outcast kids tend not to fit well. And the honest reality is that they are not terribly appealing to us either. Few of us aspire to have a youth group full of them. We fall into the very trap that Scripture warns against:

"Dear brothers, how can you claim that you belong to the Lord Jesus Christ, the Lord of glory, if you show favoritism to rich people and look down on poor people? If a man comes into your church dressed in expensive clothes and with valuable gold rings on his fingers, and at the same moment another man comes in who is poor and dressed in threadbare clothes, and you make a lot of fuss over the rich man and give him the best seat in the house and say to the poor man, 'You can stand over there if you like or else sit on the floor'—well, judging a man by his wealth shows that you are guided by wrong motives" (James 2:1-4, The Living Bible).

Yes, our own prejudices are exposed when we begin taking seriously the biblical command to treat everyone equally, especially those who are lowly in the eyes of the world.

THE CHURCH'S MOMENT?

This may be the most opportune moment the church has seen for reaching fringe youth. Thankfully, many kids today are dissatisfied with the call to "be nice church kids" as many of their predecessors were. They are looking for something far more revolutionary. William Strauss and Neil Howe in their book *The Fourth Turning: An American Prophecy,* describe this millennial generation of teenagers as being "doers" who possess the desire and ability to accomplish radical things for the Kingdom of God.[4]

Thousands of today's young people are signing up for Third-world mission trips, staying sexually pure, and even witnessing to friends. These are all wonderful, but we mustn't let them off so easily.

The last words spoken by Jesus before his ascension were, "You will receive power when the Holy Spirit comes on you; and you will be my witnesses in Jerusalem, and in all Judea and Samaria, and to the ends of the earth" (Acts 1:8). For the typical high school student, Jerusalem represents those friends who are most like them and those who they encounter every day. This is where effective ministry must always begin. Witnessing to friends and vowing to stay abstinent are both important elements of an impacting ministry in Jerusalem.

Judea represents the broader context of those who surround us and are in need—the homeless in our community, the shut-ins who reside at the nursing homes, and the children who live in a nearby orphanage. Judea is the "home missions" for our teenagers. And, of course, the ends of the earth represents the exciting two-week summer mission trip to Guatemala.

But what about Samaria? Where is that for the Christian teenager? Samaria is that section of the cafeteria where outcast teens sit embarrassingly isolated and alone day after day. It's the front seat of a school bus where occupants receive the routine brunt of spitwads and stinging rubber bands. It's the back row of a classroom where girls are badgered and mocked for their physical appearance. It's that area where kids who dress in trench coats congregate but are actively shunned by everyone else. Just as in the first century, it's the area "good" people try hard to avoid.

Samaria represents that place where those who are despised by the dominant culture reside. The most forgotten and neglected mission field of Christians, it was always at the forefront of Jesus' mind and actions. John 4:4 says, "Now he had to go through Samaria." Jesus was compelled to go there, though every other Jew of the day took great pains to avoid it altogether.

It is worth noting that after Jesus' ascension, the early church continued to avoid Samaria. That is, until widespread persecution broke out and drove them there as Acts 8 describes. Still today, as long as we remain tied to the dominant culture, we'll always be tempted to avoid Samaria for treading there threatens our good standing and reputation with the world. Sadly, persecution still seems to be the only thing that sends us into Samaria.

We simply cannot fulfill the Great Commission without venturing into Samaria. Standing up for righteousness must happen in the brutal hallways of our schools before it can happen across the world. As Mother Teresa observed, "The biggest disease today is not leprosy or tuberculosis, but rather the feeling of being unwanted, uncared for and deserted by everybody."

A PREREQUISITE

For such a radical thing as "going to Samaria" to happen, God must first begin to break our hearts as well as the hearts of our kids. We must see the parable of the Good Samaritan as a message pointed directly at us. We must recognize our own guilt in either failing to prevent or failing to provide help to these kids. Then we must be trained and mobilized in how to reach these sorts of kids. As this begins to happen, our teens, youth groups, and schools will be transformed by the power of the gospel.

Is there a risk? Sure. What would happen if we actively recruited the outcasts of our schools? There is little doubt they would come, but how might some of our other students respond? Would they leave? Perhaps some would. But it is far riskier to hear another parable of Jesus told in contemporary language:

I was picked on and you said nothing. I was excluded again and again, and you didn't invite me either. I was chased home from the school bus day after day while you silently watched. They humiliated me in front of everyone and you didn't care. Depart from me for I never knew you. "I tell you the truth, whatever you did not do for one of the least of these, you did not do for me" (Matthew 25:45).

a new type
of at-risk
teenager

Due to outbreaks of school violence, interest in troubled youth has peaked dramatically in the last few years. This is a sad reality for many reasons. School violence was not invented in 1996 when Barry Loukaitis fatally shot one teacher and two students in Moses Lake, Washington. In the 1992-1993 school year, fifty people were murdered in public schools, but because they were primarily in urban settings and involved low-income minority youth, the public outcry was much less pronounced.

Most youth trends originate in our inner cities a decade or so before becoming commonplace in suburbs and rural communities. Inner city youth violence skyrocketed in the early 1980s with the epidemic of drug use and the breakdown of the nuclear family. Crack cocaine was able to accomplish something neither slavery nor poverty could do. It caused many inner city mothers to abandon their children.

While drugs destroyed many urban families in the 1980s, rampant materialism and the quest for the American dream may be the most serious new threat to children. As sociologist Ellen Key warned a century ago, parents who direct most of their energy toward attaining wealth will raise degenerate children as surely as if those parents were addicted to alcohol or opium.

While it has not always been necessary for teachers, youth pastors, and clergy to be trained in how to minister to troubled teenagers, this is no longer the case. Today it is essential. One study commissioned by the Carnegie Council on Adolescent Development warned that one in four teenagers is extremely vulnerable to multiple high-risk behaviors, and another one in four is at moderate risk. In other words, half of America's adolescents are now considered to be at risk for serious problems and dangerous lifestyles! The report concluded that today's children are susceptible to "a vortex of new risks...almost unknown to their parents or grandparents."[1]

In 1990 the Search Institute surveyed approximately fifty thousand sixth through twelfth grade youth in mostly small Midwestern communities and found that only one in ten met a set of criteria for "optimal healthy development."[2]

AN EMERGING CATEGORY OF TROUBLED TEENAGERS

When I began in Christian youth work in the early 1980s, I was taught that students fell into three basic categories. The first category contained the popular kids: athletes, cheerleaders, and homecoming kings and queens. These were considered the leaders of their schools. The second held the masses—not particularly good kids, not particularly bad, just average. I was a part of that group. The third category was comprised of the druggies, hoodlums, and general troublemakers.

CATEGORIES OF TEENS

Category 1	Popular kids
Category 2	Average kids
Category 3	At-risk kids

"If you want to establish a solid high school ministry," we were told, "go after kids in the first category. If you can get the varsity quarterback and head cheerleader, kids in both categories one and two will follow." Nothing was ever said about the third category, confirming our assumption that you didn't particularly want these kids in your youth group anyway.

Certainly, children in the more elite upper class deserve the attention of youth pastors as much as anyone else. And perhaps their seeming perfection is a burden much stronger than many realize. Judy, a beautiful seventeen-year-old girl, for example, laments that her physical attractiveness has left her wondering if boys know who she *really* is.

Likewise, the quarterback on the football team, whose demanding father understands nothing short of perfection, feels as much like a failure as anyone else. The advanced-placement calculus student hefts the millstone of his gift in late-night study sessions, preparing once more to "prove" his worth through intellectual excellence. There are tremendous needs in every category of teens, but to target *only* the best and brightest is wrong.

Then there is the third category of at-risk kids. Our ministry, like many others, concentrates primarily on them. While they have a myriad of needs, many of these young people have far more adults interacting with them than the kids in the first two categories. Special education teachers, counselors, group care workers, and a host of others focus attention solely on this group.

Surprising to some, many in this third group are actually very effective leaders, albeit negative ones. A large percentage represent subcultures, like that of the hip-hop culture, which are attracting more and more mainstream kids. No longer representative only of a violent urban subculture, popular clothing styles now originate more from the street gangs of Los Angeles, Chicago, and New York City than from Calvin Klein designers. In fact, according to the Wall Street Journal, some designers of sneakers now do market testing among young New York City offenders before beginning mass-scale manufacturing and marketing to the larger youth market. In some ways, these kids are leading the youth culture at large.

Yet there is a new, quiet, emerging type of troubled teenager who sits in the middle. He or she has not yet been diagnosed as at risk, and thus not exposed to the services directed toward many of the more obvious rebels. They are not part of the two leadership groups on either side of them, but are more or less drifting with no clear sense of purpose or direction. Though I have worked with at-risk teenagers intensely for nearly two decades, almost none of what we know about traditional troubled teenagers fits the profile of the kids we're talking about in this book.

This child often seethes inwardly and undetected until erupting more violently than those we might expect it from. This is the youngster who lives down the street, who sits quietly alone in the cafeteria, who may even show up once or twice at youth group functions. Tragically, next to nothing is being to done to actively pursue and reach him or her. On school campuses, such kids are modern-day lepers—disconnected and alienated from the mainstream of adolescent youth culture. And let's face it, we in youth work have not been tripping over each other to minister to them either. How do we best reach out to such kids? First we need to better understand them.

It seems that there are two major types of troubled youth today. There is the traditional at-risk youth—those usually residing in the third category of young people—whose destructive behavior can usually be spotted early on. Then there is this emerging troubled teenager whose problems often remain masked until later in adolescence. This young person most often fits in this second category of kids we have been discussing.

TRADITIONAL AT-RISK YOUTH

Adolescent psychologist James Garbarino points out that there are not one or two primary risk factors that influence a young person toward violence, but eight or nine different risk factors, each carrying about the same degree of influence. It is the accumulation of these—four or more—that tend to push young people over the edge.[3]

For example, University of Michigan psychologist Arnold Sameroff tested the IQ scores of eleven-year-old children who possessed none of these risk factors. As a group, they had an average IQ of 119 versus the national average of 100. Kids with one risk factor averaged 116. Those with two averaged 113, and those with three averaged 110. What happened when four risk factors were introduced? Based on the obvious pattern one would reason it might drop to 107, but in actuality their average IQ plummeted to 96.[4] Kids can juggle one, two, or even three risk factors, but the accumulation of four or more overwhelms and devastates them.

The vast majority of traditional at-risk youth possess risk factors such as coming from a family with a history of criminal violence, being a victim of abuse or neglect, living in a violent neighborhood, and abusing alcohol and drugs. A recent report released about juvenile offenders in my home state of Massachusetts revealed that 44 percent of them had been stabbed or shot, and 35 percent had personally witnessed another person being killed.[5]

It is not surprising that that up to 40 percent of these teenagers met the diagnostic criteria for post-traumatic stress disorder. These children have experienced more trauma by age sixteen than most of us will encounter in an entire lifetime.

Fifteen-year-old José expressed this painful reality in the following prayer request he handed one of our detention Bible-study leaders recently:

> *Please pray for my friend Jared. He hung himself Sunday. I pray that he made it to heaven. Please pray my dad comes home from jail in thirty days and my HIV test comes back with what God wanted it to be.*

The remedy for kids like José is intense adult intervention like that described by the Apostle Paul in 1 Corinthians 4:15, "For though you have countless guides in Christ, you do not have many fathers. For I became your father in Christ Jesus through the gospel" (Revised Standard Version). These kids need to be re-parented. I wrote extensively about how to reach such youth in an earlier book, *At Risk: Bringing Hope to Hurting Teenagers* (Group Publishing).

Traditional at-risk youth don't tend to assimilate well into traditional youth groups. One reason is that they have had far more life experience than most youth group kids. Obviously, witnessing a homicide firsthand places one in an entirely different category of life experience than the average teen. This doesn't mean they are any more mature, but trying to integrate them with kids whose biggest problem may be not having a date for the prom is a bit of a mismatch.

Another reason that traditional youth groups sometimes don't work well for these kids is that the at-risk guys pose an immediate threat to the rest of the boys in the youth group. Suddenly the boys are in competition with the at-risk guys for the youth group girls. And youth group girls tend to have a fascination with guys who are on the edge.

For these reasons most traditional at-risk kids tend to fit much better into the college age groups at church rather than with the youth group. Here boys are not a threat to one another, they have more in common when it comes to life experiences, and there are not as many potentially damaging boy/girl relationships to develop.

THE SECOND TYPE OF AT-RISK TEENAGER

The troubled teenagers who reside in the middle category of kids don't fit many of the descriptions of traditional at-risk youth. Many of their problems may not even surface until they are well into their teenage years. Perhaps that is largely because many of them come from intact families, live in healthier neighborhoods, and have fared reasonably well in school. Such supports tend to hold kids together longer when they might otherwise drift toward the fringe.

Researchers have confirmed that two of the risk factors contributing to violent behavior are simply being thirteen to fifteen years old and being male.[6] Thus, when an adolescent boy experiences extreme peer rejection—a common theme present in every recent incident of homicidal school violence—one can begin to envision how some kids go off the deep end.

While we have been referring mostly to boys, that doesn't mean girls are somehow immune to bullying and peer rejection or responding to it in destructive ways. While boys who are bullied tend to act out in more violent anti-social ways, girls are much more prone to internalize their pain. As a result, many develop eating disorders, overt depression, or self-destructive behavior.[7]

Listen to the pain contained in the journal entries of Kip Kinkel, the fifteen-year-old who, shortly after going off the anti-depressant drug, Prozac, shot and killed his parents and two classmates in 1998:

> *"I sit here all alone. I am always alone. I don't know who I am. I want to be something I can never be. I try so hard every day. But in the end, I hate myself for what I've become. The only reason I stay alive is because of hope. Every time I talk to her [a girl he likes], I have a small amount of hope. But then she will tear it right down. It feels like my heart is breaking. I feel like everyone is against me. Please. Someone, help me. All I want is something small. Nothing big. I just want to be happy. It is clear that no one will help me. Oh God, I am so close to killing people. So close."[8]*

One cannot underestimate the power of peer relationships when it comes to teenagers. Feeling rejected by peers is a curse almost unequaled in the mind of a young person, as expressed by one eighth-grader: "When you're at this stage, it's all about fitting in. And when you don't, you're a social outcast and a target."

While caring adults are important for these kids, positive peers are just as critical. They desperately long for and need authentic and embracing peer relationships, making them prime candidates for any solid youth group. In fact, such a connection can mean the difference between life and death for them, if not literally, at least emotionally.

a culture
of cruelty

Whenever the role of bullying arises with respect to school violence, many adults respond, "Come on, we were picked on as kids, too, but we never chose to kill people because of it." True enough, and of the millions of kids who are bullied, only a few strike out or commit destructive acts. The vast majority suffer without stooping to this level of vindictive retaliation.

Obviously there are a myriad of issues beyond simple bullying that contribute to some of the more heinous crimes we have witnessed recently—issues that neither this nor any other book can reduce to a simple formula. But while every generation has had its share of bullies and their victims, the culture surrounding today's teens has changed dramatically. Following are some of the factors that contribute to today's kids being much more prone toward violence:

1. REVENGE IN VOGUE — The great majority of movies and television programs today glorify revenge, making heroes out of the underdog who has finally had enough and strikes back, proving "Vengeance is mine. *I* will repay."

The disturbing part is that the ends always seem to justify the means. Any act of retribution is acceptable for the one who has been victimized. From Rambo to RoboCop, the message is clear: Mass destruction is but a small price to pay to avenge those who have been exploited.

2. VIDEO VIOLENCE — Ready access to violent video games desensitizes children to violence the same way that our military prepares combat soldiers for killing.[1] Children are affected in two ways. First, the number of murders they see inoculates them against the horrors of violence. Second, through participating in simulated violence they begin to mentally rehearse such activities, actually increasing the chances of such events occurring.[2]

3. EASY ACCESS TO GUNS — Nearly half the households in America have at least one gun, and two-thirds of teenagers say they could obtain a gun within an hour if they so desired.[3] The difference between the number of firearm-related homicides in the United States compared with the rest of the industrialized world is startling. In 1985, handguns were responsible for the deaths of nearly eighty-one hundred Americans. The next closest country that year was Japan with forty-six.[4]

4. TOO MUCH, TOO SOON — Adolescence has always been a time of exploration and pushing the limits. For some, living on the edge is comprised of skipping an occasional class or jumping off a bridge into a river. But for many teenagers like Courtney, who Patricia Hersch describes in her book *A Tribe Apart*, the boundaries of acceptability have become far too broad. "Only fourteen, Courtney has had sex, has carried on a full-blown social life in the middle of the night, smoked cigarettes and pot, cut classes, been with somebody who 'stole' his parents' car. By her freshman year, she was bored with legitimate school activities."[5]

5. SPIRITUALLY DEPRAVED — Researchers know that faith-based programs work for troubled youth. Studies have shown that young people who are spiritually anchored respond better to trauma and exhibit less depression, casual sex, substance abuse, and suicide.[6] When spirituality is absent, however, kids can easily fall prey to fatalistic thinking and a loss of purpose.

Add to all this the fact that peers become the greatest influence on youngsters during adolescence, and when they feel unaccepted by them their world begins to crumble. One can begin to imagine how some kids who are picked on day in and day out can get to the point where they see no way out but to inflict violence upon themselves or others. The point is not to excuse the vindictive actions of kids, but to better understand how kids can get to such a point.

Fifteen-year-old Jesse explains it this way, "If you go to school and people make fun of you every day and you don't have friends, it drives you to insanity." Kids like Jesse tend to survive when they have the right external supports around them, but when other risk factors accumulate, that sense of "insanity" can take a dangerous course.

WHY KIDS ARE BULLIED

While no two kids are exactly the same, the major reasons kids are picked on tend to be similar. In short, it is anything that makes them stand out from the mainstream or reveals a weakness or vulnerability. For most teenagers, possessing any of these qualities is a curse worse than death.

There are at least five common traits that tend to make kids susceptible to extreme bullying by peers: undesirable physical characteristics, countercultural lifestyles, sexuality issues, extreme inwardness, and challenging temperaments. Each is described in more detail below.

Undesirable Physical Characteristics

Sara often wondered whether a fate worse than being overweight existed. The square-jawed seventh-grader worried constantly about her obesity, her anxiety amplified by the constant ridicule she received at school. A feeling of self-hatred filled her as she looked in the mirror each night. She believed that she would never experience love, mostly because she was not worthy of it.

Students frequently called her "Fido," after a fat, lazy dog from a story read during her language arts class. The other title she came to recognize was "pig," spoken quietly but audibly, even during class. After Christmas vacation, she told her mother she did not want to go back to school. "Just ignore them. They're only names," she was told.

Sara's one joy in an otherwise horrific school experience was choir. She had a beautiful, well-trained voice. Despite her obvious talent, fellow choir members still teased and taunted Sara about her appearance. She was willing to put up with this irritation in exchange for the transcendent beauty, the feeling of being taken out of herself provided by blended voices at certain magical moments.

Her tenacity eventually paid off, as the director nominated Sara to receive a special award. It was an extraordinary honor for a "lowly" seventh grader to receive such recognition in such a competitive, high-powered school.

As Sara walked toward the stage in the honors assembly, several boys in the front row started the snorting sounds she had grown accustomed to hearing. Many others took up the chant and, until the principal hushed everyone with a sharp word, a chorus of snorts, oinks, and "Fidos" filled the auditorium. Disconcerted, Sara misstepped in climbing to the stage and fell noisily into an undignified heap. The resulting laughter echoing off the gymnasium walls sounded like thunder in her ears.

Humiliated to the core, Sara determined to lose weight or die trying. She applied the same discipline to her body that she had to developing her musical talent. As her weight dropped, for the first time in her life she received one compliment after another about her appearance. Suddenly, boys who had once studiously ignored her began to pay attention.

Like so many with eating disorders, the sense of power and control over her own body achieved by food refusal became euphoric for Sara. But no matter how much weight she lost, Sara never really believed in her heart that she was thin enough.

Midway through her ninth grade year, Sara discovered the short-lived but intense feeling of acceptance provided by conferring sexual favors. From that point on, she filled the emptiness in her soul with willpower over food, momentary acceptance through promiscuity, and the use of amphetamines which also helped her stay thin. After Sara was hospitalized, her counselor asked her to name one thing that she liked about herself. Pausing for nearly two full minutes, she responded, "At least I never feel hungry anymore."

Sara is now in her early twenties. She has inflicted permanent damage to her body and continues to be in and out of residential eating disorder programs. But like most teenagers, she was willing to pay whatever price it took to fit in, regardless of the personal cost involved.

Polly Nichols describes the sort of bullying that Sara endured as lookism, namely the ranking of persons by superficial physical appearances.[7] Though more subtle than sexism or racism, lookism is also more pervasive.

The great majority of young people report being dissatisfied with how they look. From early adolescence, they are preoccupied with physical appearance in themselves and others. Unfortunately, when grave importance is attached to random human differences, superficial traits become the measure of the worth of self and others.

Had students hurled epithets about race or physical disability at Sara as she walked across the auditorium stage, adults would have held them accountable. But under the excuse that "kids will be kids," massive amounts of verbal abuse occur every day. Four out of five episodes of teasing and taunting that occur between middle and high school students involve insults about body appearance.[8] Equally tragic, young people who begin to evaluate themselves against such destructive standards ultimately become mired in self-hatred.

All teenagers are subject to this sort of destructive thinking. Psychologist Alfred Adler popularized the term "inferiority complex" to describe twentieth-century adolescents who constantly compare themselves to others and feel they do not measure up. Of course, whenever we compare ourselves to others we always come up on the short end.

Several years ago I was asked to speak at a Christian youth retreat on the topic of self-esteem. After sizing up the group, I couldn't imagine how such an attractive group of young people could struggle with any negative issues of self-image. So I asked them to write anonymously on three-by-five-inch cards how they felt about themselves.

I was shocked to discover that nine out of ten said they either hated themselves or greatly disliked themselves. During the next session, I reported the results and asked them to write down why they saw themselves in such a negative light. The top three responses were: *I'm ugly. I'm stupid. I don't have any friends.*

A study was referenced in Seventeen magazine that surveyed the most beautiful high school girls in America. They discovered that 97 percent of them felt they were ugly, an even higher percentage than the general population of teenage girls.

The media plays an enormous role in perpetuating this sense of insecurity. For example, in 1995, 3 percent of girls on the island of Fiji suffered from bulimia. That was the year television arrived. Within just three short years, the rate of bulimia among teenage girls had jumped to 17 percent.[9]

Possessing the necessary elements of popularity is out of the reach of more and more teenagers today. Less than 5 percent of girls fall within the height and weight prescriptions of acceptability, according to television and movies in which near-anorexic models are routinely airbrushed to narrow hips and lengthen legs for a still thinner look. Perhaps most tragic is that the effects of such images are reaching younger and younger children. A recent study found that 39 percent of girls in grades five to eight said they were on a diet; 13 percent of those girls said they had already binged and purged, symptoms of bulimia.[10]

While lookism is most pervasive among girls, frustration over not being able to live up to physical images is becoming increasingly more common among boys as well. The macho images of muscular bodies are out of reach for most men, let alone boys struggling through puberty. While advertisements showing beautiful models project images nearly impossible for girls to live up to, retailers like Abercrombie and Fitch are marketing the bodies of boys in an equally aggressive and degrading manner.

The appearance of toys like G. I. Joe has changed dramatically over the years. While the toys used to more closely simulate real-life figures, that is no longer the case. In 1964, G. I. Joe had 12.2-inch biceps. By 1974 they were 15.2 inches. They had grown to 16.4 by 1984, and in 1998, had reached 28.4 inches—larger than any bodybuilder in history.[11]

Countercultural Lifestyles

"My elementary school teachers always praised me for my intelligence and creativity, but when I got into middle school, suddenly it was a detriment," recalls nineteen-year-old Adam. "I wore my hair long when everyone else's was short. I was hyper, loved to skateboard, and was into a whole different kind of music than everyone else. It was like I had committed the ultimate crime. Everyone picked on me, nonstop.

"The church I was attending with my mom started saying that I was a Satanist because of my music and how I dressed. 'Fine,' I thought, so I dropped out and actually started getting into the devil. Of course, that just made me even more of an outcast at home and in school.

"By seventh grade I was tired of being the outsider, so I cut my hair and got rid of my wild clothes. It was amazing. Almost immediately kids started accepting me more. The same kids who used to chase me home after school and beat me up were suddenly inviting me to their parties. Even the girls who had nothing to do with me were now talking to me. It was with these kids that I started getting into marijuana heavily. In my school, the popular crowd lived their whole lives around smoking weed. But I always knew they only liked me because I was dressing and acting like them. That made me real angry underneath.

"After a while, I started hanging out with some other kids who were into military stuff, and sure enough, I was once again on the outside. It made me just say, 'Screw 'em.' I started getting into the army stuff real big. I shaved my head and wore only military fatigues. We would train each weekend, paint our faces, do work on our forts, and devise tactics for the coming week. Our dream was to get into the Army or Navy and kill people.

"The only thing I took with me from my former life was my drug habit. We were getting high three or four times a day. Everyone avoided us, but talked a lot about us behind our backs because they were afraid of us. We were deep into the martial arts, and I remember overhearing one kid talking about us. I came up to him, looked him straight in eyes and told him, 'If you got something to say to me, say it to my face. If I hear you talking behind my back again, I'll kill you.' He was real scared. I remember how good it made me feel to have such control over people and to be able to torture them through fear. Even my father, who had always beaten me, stayed away from me out of fear.

"In the ninth grade I met a girl named Jennifer at a concert. We got real close. She even told me about how her eighteen-year-old brother had raped her when she was thirteen, something she had never told anybody else. She said that sometimes I scared her, too, especially with all the hate that I had, and with my drug use. So I stopped both.

"Jennifer was my morning, noon, night, and weekend. She would either sneak into my house, or I would sneak into hers almost every night. My parents were too busy to notice, and I think they were just glad that I had once again changed my image. Now I was into the beatnik lifestyle. I wore old baggy clothes and started playing the drums. 'You've really changed Adam; you no longer want to kill people,' Jennifer boasted. 'You only want me and your drums.'

"After being together for two and a half years, Jennifer broke up with me for another guy. After that I went into a deep depression and became very suicidal."

Kids like Adam try on lifestyles, going from one to another like many of us try on clothes. But just because someone dresses in black, Gothic style doesn't necessarily mean he completely embraces its counterculture ideology. Likewise, a girl experimenting with a Wiccan lifestyle hasn't necessarily sold herself to the devil, though there is impending danger whenever one opens oneself to pagan influences.

Many kids make radical changes in lifestyles out of an attempt to draw love and attention from their parents by shocking them. Nearly all children experiment with lifestyles and issues of identities. What often differentiates them is the degree of experimentation and the number of possibilities they "see" around them or in the media.

Kids like Adam who have been rejected from the mainstream of youth culture are desperately seeking a place to fit in. Don't be too quick to cast them aside as lost or too far gone based upon the countercultural styles they embrace. Most of the time, it is whoever loves and embraces them most genuinely who determines where they will end up.

Fortunately for Adam, Christian friends reached out to him shortly after he and Jennifer broke up. I met him at a Christian camp I was speaking at when he surrendered his life to Christ. Two years later when I interviewed him for this book, he was still flourishing in his faith and in the fellowship of "true friends," as he put it.

Sexuality Issues

Research confirms that the most common method of school bullying is sexist intimidation. Girls tend to be picked on for one of two reasons. First are those who are ridiculed because they are seen as physically unattractive. Others are picked on because they are seen as being attractive, often developing ahead of their peers. Both groups are usually bullied because of rumors of sexual promiscuity.[12]

In 1993, The American Association of University Women released a report called "Hostile Hallways: The AAUW Survey on Sexual Harassment in America's Schools." The report stated that four out of five girls and three out of four boys had experienced some sort of sexual harassment in school. The National School Safety Center News Service called sexual harassment the most "overlooked and underreported offense today."[13]

Boys who do not fit the macho social image are the greatest recipients of cruel attacks. Those who may be physically smaller or who prefer art or music to sports are always susceptible. Any youth who appears unlikely to fight back is also a target. Bullies have a way of finding weaker kids, pushing them around, and calling them demeaning names like "sissy" or "faggot." According to one study, the average high school student hears twenty-five such slurs each day.[14]

Many youth struggle with their sexual identity during their teenage years. Experimentation with those of the same sex is not uncommon in adolescence. Profuse bullying over such issues or homosexual labeling by peers only adds to the confusion kids are already facing, driving them further from the mainstream.

A full one-third of teenage and young-adult suicides of both boys and girls involve the struggle with concerns about whether or not they are homosexual.[15] Sadly, we in the Christian community have typically been the most paranoid about such struggles and among the first to throw stones, rather than loving unconditionally and guiding them through these times of struggle and confusion. Because of this, many fringe kids do not think of the church as the first place to go in search of love, acceptance, and healing.

RAY

Ray faithfully attended our detention center Bible studies for all four years of his incarceration. Several times he had even expressed strong interest in becoming a minister.

It was during the final six weeks of Ray's life that I began to observe some troubling signs. He quit attending Bible study and appeared quiet, distant, and depressed on those rare occasions when I would happen upon him in the hallway.

Perhaps it was that he would be turning twenty-one and the state would be forced to release him. And certainly the fact that his father had just been released from prison and was now living back home with Ray's younger sister might have contributed to his melancholic disposition. Ray had been sexually molested by his father and was quite sure that his father would pick up with his sister where he had left off with Ray.

Then there was the question that the other members of the Bible study raised one of those weeks when Ray was absent. "It's a sin to be homosexual, right?"

"The Bible does say it's a sin to act on homosexual temptations just as it is to act on heterosexual ones outside the confines of marriage. While acting on the temptation is a sin, struggling with the temptation is not," I pointed out, not really understanding what was behind their line of questioning. Then we looked in Romans 2 and noted how homosexuality was listed in the same camp as greed, deceit, and gossip.

It turned out that Ray had recently been struggling with his sexual identity during his counseling sessions. Rather than helping him sort through issues from the past, his clinician urged him to come public with the declaration that he was gay. As he began testing the waters with his peers, he met harsh resistance, especially from his fellow Bible study companions.

Nobody will ever know which of these issues finally brought Ray to such a point of desperation, but his was the first successful suicide attempt in the fifty-year history of that juvenile facility. He hung himself by tying a sock over the hinge of his bedroom door, five feet off the ground.

While we should not advocate for homosexual sins any more than other sexual sins, neither should we tolerate gay bashing, crude jokes, or name-calling from those in our youth groups.[16] Kids can quickly sense the pulse of a group. They instinctively know whether or not it is a place where they can openly struggle with significant life issues.

I recently attended a two-day retreat for Christian youth workers. While hanging out with other youth workers, I heard three different homosexual jokes and degrading slurs. This is unacceptable for any Christian, but especially for those desiring to reach teenagers.

The world of today's teenagers is much more tolerant of homosexuality than the one we grew up in. Most of us would be quite surprised at just how prevalent homosexuals are in today's schools. In 1999 there were more than six hundred formal gay and lesbian clubs on American high school campuses, up from fewer than one hundred the year before.[17]

Thus, many kids who hear Christians speaking in berating terms conclude that the church is completely out of touch with what is going on in the world. Others conclude that gay bashing is acceptable behavior for the Christian and join in themselves. A good percentage of bigotry through the ages has been done in the name of Christianity. But even more tragically, it confirms to kids that a church youth group is not a place where they can openly struggle with sensitive matters. Hence, they stay far away, either emotionally or physically.

Issues of sexuality loom large in the minds of teenagers. Research indicates that by age sixteen, one in four girls will have experienced some sort of sexual abuse, as will one in seven boys.[18] Of course, the real numbers are much higher, as only 61 percent of cases are actually reported. Perhaps this is because in 80 percent of sexual abuse cases, the perpetrator is a family member, relative, friend or neighbor.[19]

Our culture has contributed radically to the enormous confusion in our young people regarding sexuality. In one survey of sixth to ninth graders, 65 percent of boys and 57 percent of girls believed that it would be acceptable for a man to force a woman to have sex if they had been dating for six months.[20] Hence, it is not surprising that one in three teenage girls will experience violence in a dating relationship before she graduates from high school.[21]

As a result, discussions on sexual abuse and alternative sexual lifestyles must be added to the regular curriculum of youth groups, just as we have done with the traditional topics of love, sex, and dating.

Extreme Inwardness

Research has shown that it is often the cautious, sensitive, quiet individuals who classmates tend to prey upon most. In short, anyone who doesn't defend him or herself becomes highly susceptible.

Sadly, those very qualities that characterize good friends and effectiveness in the helping professions must be unlearned or compromised to ensure survival in our schools. Instead of thriving and being affirmed for their sensitivity, schoolyard antics make these students prone to anxiety attacks, stress-related symptoms, and depression. One such kid expressed these feelings, saying, "I felt like the whole world was caving in on me, like I just couldn't take it anymore."

Because most victims of bullying tend to be more anxious and insecure than the average student, they often respond by crying (at least in lower grades) and withdrawing. Feeling lonely and abandoned in school, many say they do not have a single good friend in their class.[22] They see the world through tainted glasses that amplify the negative and reduce the positive.

Of course, not all children who hide their pain get to the place where they destroy themselves or others. Most grow up and move beyond the tumultuous adolescent years. But some have suffered so many losses that they are unwilling or unable to deal with any more sadness. Some losses are obvious, such as the death of a friend or family member. For others, it is the combination of many small losses that accumulate and overwhelm them. These children desperately need others to help them develop the courage to master loss and sadness in the circumstances of daily living. Without help, these children can fall into depression.

Not only were the perpetrators of school violence at the turn of the century victims of school bullying, each of them also suffered from some sort of depression.[23] Sadly, depression has become far too common in our day. Child psychiatrist David Fassler estimates that more than one in four youngsters will experience a serious episode of depression by the time he or she reaches the age of eighteen.[24] This is a dramatic increase over the 2 percent average rate of serious depression in the 1960s.[25] A "Catch-22," kids in this state become even greater targets for schoolyard bullies who thrive on exploiting the weak.

Challenging Temperaments

Kids who are hyperactive or display other qualities that differentiate them from their peers or are difficult to be around suffer more than their share of peer abuse.

MITCH

One of the kids who stands out in the memory bank of my junior and senior high school years is Mitch. While the terms *attention-deficit disorder, disruptive behavior disorder, oppositional defiant disorder, conduct disorder,* and *attention-deficit hyperactive disorder* were not so familiar in the mid-1970s, I'm sure Mitch had them all.

In elementary school, both teachers and peers saw Mitch as a bright, creative, sensitive kid. Unfortunately, life changes completely with the introduction of junior high school. Suddenly, the rules of acceptability change and, unfortunately, it is the bullies who function as peer police enforcing the new social code.

Within the first month of junior high, the roster of who was in and who was out was being clearly established. It was quickly evident that Mitch's qualities placed him about as far down as one could get. There was one particular characteristic that Mitch possessed that would be his doom for the next six years.

He could tolerate teasing and ridicule only up to a certain point before he would eventually blow up. Books would fly and a desk would tip over, followed by the slamming of a classroom door and the sound of feet stomping down the hallway. All the while, a stream of profanity could be heard at the highest of decibels, culminating with the words, "I'm going to kill you!"—a phrase taken much more seriously today than it was back then.

I was sitting in a classroom several rooms away the first time this event occurred in our school. In the middle of class, scores of us ceased what we were doing to listen in bewilderment. The boys who brought Mitch to that point were ecstatic. These are the sorts of rewards for which junior high boys live. And so the ritual went on to become an all too familiar weekly to biweekly event. We smiled and chuckled every time a classroom door slammed as we anticipated the words that would follow.

Most of us weren't the designated instigators, but we all enjoyed it nonetheless. Perhaps it was the fact that profanity was being blurted out throughout the school in a way that administrators were powerless to curb. Maybe it was that Mitch brought a sense of excitement to an otherwise mundane school experience. Or perhaps it was just the assurance that Mitch provided us that we weren't the lowest rungs on the ladder of the junior high pecking order.

As I look back on my adolescent days, one of my biggest regrets is that I did nothing to befriend or defend Mitch. In fact, out of our entire class of seven hundred students, no one did. I don't even recall seeing anyone disciplined for the cruel and inhumane treatment that was relentlessly heaped upon Mitch. The badgering and belittlement continued unabated right up through high school graduation. What other sector of society would tolerate such behavior? Truly, there are few places more cruel than a junior or senior high school campus.

AT A CROSSROADS

We stand at a critical crossroads in American youth culture. No longer confined to troubled families or poverty-stricken neighborhoods, teenage violence has moved mainstream. And while the current school bombings and shootings may be a temporary fad, the personal and cultural issues driving these heinous crimes make it unlikely that the violence will subside. Why has it taken such tragedies to wake us to the call to do what we should have been doing all along?

Much less obvious than those who act out in radical ways are the thousands of ostracized kids who reside in every community—kids who feel left out of the mainstream of youth culture. Most of them suffer so quietly that they are almost invisible to the rest of us.

Is your youth group reaching kids like these? If not, is it ready to? Is it ready to begin with simple acts of kindness, but then to move toward

actively reaching out and including outcast young people in their programs? Is it ready to lead hungry and hurting hearts into hope and healing
through the power of the gospel, and then to equip and release them back
into ministry to others? That's what the next section is about. But before
going any further, take a moment to pray right now that the youth group
you represent might begin to catch such a powerful vision.

risk
IN OUR MIDST

PART 2

where
are
we?

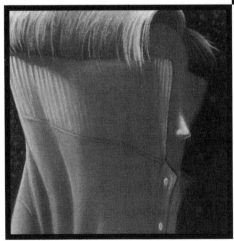

getting beyond the barriers

Jeremy was the first full-time youth pastor First Baptist Church had ever had. He arrived excited, with a passion to reach lost kids. Throughout the interview process, everyone saw this as a plus. But, as is so often the case, each person involved in the process had his or her own idea of what "reaching lost kids" actually meant.

To Jim, the chairman of the search committee, it was a church growth strategy. As new youth became involved, their parents would also begin attending; eventually becoming committed members themselves.

Robin, another member of the search committee, had put her own son Andy in that category of "lost kids." Andy had wanted nothing to do with the church since entering high school. Robin was excited about finally having a full-time youth pastor on board who could spend time with kids like Andy, who needed to be brought back.

The senior pastor was not an official member of the committee but certainly had input into the process. He was excited that the church was finally committed to a second full-time person on the pastoral staff. This position was crucial to him. The last two families to leave the church did so because the Methodist church in town had a much more vibrant youth ministry. Like many parents of teenagers, these families were willing to go wherever their children felt most comfortable. As senior pastor, he could now assure visitors and regular attendees that First Baptist would be able to offer them an outstanding ministry for their teenagers.

Jeremy also had his own definition of what it meant to reach lost kids. No one foresaw just how much conflict these various approaches would bring to First Baptist Church. Instead of occupying his office at the church, Jeremy spent the majority of his time at the local high school and at the places where kids hang out. It was actually the fringe kids Jeremy began connecting with most, probably because these were the youngsters that were hungriest for adult attention.

Nobody would argue with the fact that these kids were lost and in need of the Savior, but when they began showing up at the church, trouble began to brew. The small core of youth group kids didn't click with the newcomers at all. They began complaining to their parents about how burnouts, metal heads, and outcasts were taking over their youth program.

A parent meeting with Jeremy was soon scheduled. "What do you think you're doing?" were among the first words spoken.

"We've been trying to keep our daughter away from kids like this, and now you're trying to get them together!" charged another angry father.

"I come in here Wednesday morning and the bathrooms smell like cigarette smoke, the parking lot is littered with trash, and my answering machine is filled with the complaints of angry parishioners," chimed in the pastor.

"But I thought we agreed that we wanted to reach lost kids," exclaimed Jeremy. "I've been working for months to get these kids to trust me enough to come to our youth group, and now you want me to kick them out?! What kind of a church are we?"

Within two months, Jeremy had resigned and joined a parachurch ministry, determined never to waste his time in church ministry again. First Baptist was licking their wounds as well, questioning whether they would ever take another risk like hiring a youth pastor again.

BREAKING BARRIERS

Reaching fringe kids is not an easy task. It involves much more than simply inviting such kids to our programs. Fringe and outcast kids will often come when we begin spending time with them. But then what do we do with them? Because the youth group is a microcosm of the church at large, changing the climate and focus of a youth group demands that we deal with the entire church body as well.

Therefore, assessing where we are involves more than just asking if the youth group reaches out to those beyond their walls to those who are unlike them. We must also ask how much the larger church body does the same. If the real answer is "Never, or very little," then for the youth group to begin doing so sets up an imminent clash of agendas as was revealed in the example of Jeremy.

Both parties bear responsibility in the case of First Baptist. Obviously, the church is in need of some serious reflection and examination about who they are and what their mission is, but Jeremy also bears some of the blame. It is just as big a mistake to neglect the youth of the church while bringing in an entirely different make-up of kids that makes the core group feel overwhelmed and overrun.

A FORTRESS OR A HOSPITAL?

Much of this conflict stems from a basic difference in philosophy. Is the church primarily a fortress, or is it a hospital? A large percentage of church conflicts occur around these two divergent paradigms. In reality, the church is both.

There needs to be a safe place for youth group kids to feel secure, loved, ministered to, and cared for *before* they can be expected to reach out beyond their own circle of friends. The word "sanctuary" after all, means a place of refuge or safety. Establishing such an environment is a process. It doesn't happen over night. It can take years. And the truth is, some youth groups never get there, requiring the youth leader to wait for a new crop of kids to embrace such an ethos.

Jesus poured into his disciples for more than two years before he began sending them out among the wolves. That band of twelve wasn't anxious to leave the Master's side or the companionship of one another any more than most youth groups will cherish the idea of bringing in strangers—especially when those strangers are different from them, when they are members of another fold. But Jesus possessed wisdom to know when that point of necessity had come.

We need his wisdom, for in every church or youth group there exists an energy that, when not directed outward, naturally turns inward to gossip, backbiting, and self-destruction.

Because youth tend to be a bit more malleable than adults, preparing them for such outreach is often easier than with the church at large. Yet without the backing of the senior pastor, leadership, and church community, efforts by the youth group to reach out will quickly be stymied.

Because of the potential resistance, many youth workers are tempted to ignore the difficult task of trying to integrate fringe kids into the life of the larger church. This is a fatal mistake, however, and part of the reason why so many kids drop out after high school, never to return to active church life.

When a kid's only exposure to spiritual vitality happens in the context of a youth group, what is he or she left with when they are no longer of youth group age? They have no concept of the larger body of

Christ. Even if, at some later point, they do happen to wander into a church looking to reconnect to spiritual things, the environment is so foreign to them that they seldom stay.

Below are some other barriers to effectively reaching out:

1. Core youth group kids become swayed more by the fringe kids than the other way around. Recently, I was on a national Christian radio program talking about how to reach at-risk kids. I was taken by surprise when the first question asked of me was, "So how do we keep our children away from at-risk kids?"

Though at first I was floored that the host would even ask such a question, I understood the struggle every parent faces when it comes to the friends their teenager chooses. How do we reconcile the reality of the Apostle Paul's words that "bad company corrupts good character" (1 Corinthians 15:33), with his strategy of living among them for their sake (1 Thessalonians 1:5)?

In the context of a youth group, avoid introducing great numbers of fringe kids into a shallow or fractured youth group environment. This is a recipe for disaster for both sides. Instead, begin building into the core kids a sense of what it means to be a genuine loving community. At the same time, teach that to follow Christ demands that we reach out and bring into our community those who live on the fringes of life. Ideally, it should be the youth themselves who invite such kids, not primarily the leaders. Otherwise, the youth group kids will resent newcomers and eventually drive them away.

As kids begin to invite those who may be more troubled, it is important that the troubled kids not come in such great numbers that they overtake the group, influencing it downward. Since peer pressure is inevitable, it is far better that it be positive peer pressure.

2. Core group kids drop out as kids who are lower on the scale of schoolyard hierarchy begin attending. Amy, a high school junior, was petrified by the thought of befriending some of the "geeks and freaks" in her school. Her reasoning: "I've worked for three years to break into one of the popular groups in my school. Hanging out with kids like that would undo everything!"

Every kid knows the pecking order of his or her school. According to many, at the bottom are the druggies, trendies, nerds, techies, wiggers, rednecks, and freaks. But as one young man said, "The *real* losers at the very bottom are invisible." Research confirms that 48 percent of students believe that associating with students of a lower level would result in the reduction of their own social status as well.[1]

We are all drawn to those most like us or to those we deem to be slightly above us, but such an attitude does not fare well according to Jesus. "Being in very nature God, [he] did not consider equality with God something to be grasped, but made himself nothing, taking the very nature of a servant, being made in human likeness" (Philippians 2:6-7). Reaching down, as well as up, is imperative for the believer, but that will only come as a fruit of the work of God's Spirit in our lives and in the lives of the kids we work with.

The secure kids in our youth groups must be willing to lead by reaching out to the "invisible kids." Certainly there is nothing wrong with having upper echelon kids in our youth groups. The problem comes when such kids are not willing to use their influence to help others.

3. Churches may view the influx of troubled kids as a compromise to their standard of upholding righteous behavior. Whenever I speak on the need to reach kids on the fringe, one of the first questions youth pastors ask is "How do I do what you're saying and keep my job at the same time?"

One woman told me that when she was hired, the only mandate the board gave her was to keep kids out of the fellowship hall because of the new carpet. She later learned that the "new carpet" had actually been installed seven years before. Needless to say, she had a lot of ground to cover before incorporating troubled kids into her program.

A friend who ministers to teen moms in the inner city works hard to get her girls involved in local churches. After taking them to several different services, the girls unanimously chose the one they liked best. It wasn't the place with the most dynamic preaching or even the most hip music, so she asked them what was behind their choice.

"We feel welcome there," they said.

"Why?" she asked curiously.

"Because there are ashtrays in the lobby."

For some, that would be a definite compromise. But I happen to know something about the church those girls chose. They don't advocate for smoking in any way, but they are serious about making outsiders feel welcome and it's working.

How do we both make sinners feel welcome and uphold a standard of righteousness that causes them to be drawn to Christ? Not an easy question, but one every church and youth group must be willing to wrestle with.

4. Reaching out too broadly makes a youth group eclectic, removing its distinctives and cohesiveness. There is little doubt that the majority of us feel most comfortable with people who are most like us, but that is not what the body of Christ is about. In fact, the Apostle Paul goes into painstaking detail to explain why the opposite is necessary:

"God has arranged the parts in the body, every one of them, just as he wanted them to be. If they were all one part, where would the body be? As it is, there are many parts, but one body. The eye cannot say to the hand, 'I don't need you!' And the head cannot say to the feet, 'I don't need you!' On the contrary, those parts of the body that seem to be weaker are indispensable" (1 Corinthians 12:18-22).

I am part of a small group that has been struggling with this very issue. "We're really starting to gel together and to trust one another," said one of our members. "I feel like if we start bringing in new people now, all of that could be lost." We did have a great thing going, but we had forgotten why we existed. It wasn't just for us but for the benefit of others as well.

When we eventually did invite new people, we found that it didn't take us nearly as long to get back to the same level of intimate sharing. We were able to more quickly replicate what we had learned. And newcomers, knowing their own hunger for intimacy, were eager to follow our example.

5. Reaching out can be interpreted by members of the opposite sex as being flirtatious. This is a significant issue and one that can cause more damage than any of the others we have discussed. As our youth consciously begin to reach out to others, including those of the opposite sex, it is important to educate them in how to be honest about their intentions of friendship so that their kindness is not misinterpreted as flirtation.

This can be an important learning opportunity as both girls and guys become more aware of what their actions communicate to the opposite sex. There are few things more embarrassing for young people than to realize that the girls or boys who were paying so much attention to them did not have the same level of interest as they had hoped. This only heaps more rejection and a deeper sense of abandonment and betrayal on them. The fear of being misinterpreted should never be an excuse for not extending kindness toward the opposite sex, but the primary reaching out and befriending should happen between those of the same sex.

Likewise, it is embarrassing for young people to have others taunt them, saying they are in love with Martha, who is seen as unattractive, or with Ralph, who is considered the "class geek." Because of the tremendous pressure to enforce the pecking order and to marginalize people even within youth groups, members must be tenacious about curbing such behavior.

There are ramifications when relationships do develop. Parents and parishioners become concerned about possible romantic attachments made between children who look different or come from the opposite side of the tracks.

One last issue that must be addressed concerns vulnerability. Young people who have been ostracized and rejected by peers may feel pressured into sexual activity as a means of gaining acceptance. Taking sexual advantage of vulnerable kids, while not as likely to occur in a church group, needs to be addressed nonetheless.

6. Many of these kids appear not to want our help. Kids who have been victimized tend to keep their guard up. They may be suspicious of those who suddenly seem to come on strongly. Sadly, many have already been hurt by Christians or may blame God for their predicament. As one teenager told me, "I don't believe in God. How could I believe in a God who could arrange a life as lousy as mine?" Such kids understandably hold back from jumping into something they think could cause them additional hurt and pain.

Others, like Eddie, may just be indifferent when it comes to relating with adults. Eddie was a quiet kid in high school, definitely a loner. He had always attended large schools, so it was not unusual that he skated through relatively unnoticed. I took a bit of an interest in him at a youth retreat where I was speaking. He was curiously cool toward my attempts to reach out and communicate with him though.

At first I became self-conscious, wondering if he didn't like my messages. As I inquired more about Eddie, his youth leaders expressed the same frustration. They knew very little about him except that he lived in a foster home and had come for the weekend through the invitation of a friend.

As it turned out, Eddie wasn't necessarily angry at adults; he just didn't think about them all that much. He had never related to an adult in any significant way. To him, adults were simply the ones who called the shots and they generally did so from a distance. They made decisions about things like where he and his siblings would live. They were the ones who determined what sort of work would be required of him to advance from one grade to the next. In his experience, the further one stayed away from adults, the less likely they were to notice and interfere.

PERSONAL BARRIERS

Each of the previous barriers involves the youth, youth group, or the church, but there are also more personal barriers that keep us from reaching out to outcast kids.

1. The personal cost is too high. While some kids like Eddie take all of our energy just to break through, others like Kevin can take all of our energy to break away from.

I met Kevin in my first youth-worker position. He came about halfway through the year with a friend who had been actively attending. We hit it off almost immediately. As I learned more about him, it became clear that he had been quite seriously abused, neglected, and abandoned by family members. He was living in a foster home, and the youth group was becoming his lifeblood.

In many ways, Kevin made me feel good. Here was a kid who really did have serious needs, in contrast to many of the others for whom receiving a C in calculus or spotting an emerging zit qualified as a crisis. Kevin asked for advice on matters that at times seemed almost life and death. And he appreciated every minute I invested in him.

After several months, though, I began to dread the ringing of the telephone or the doorbell for fear it would be Kevin. And more often than not, it was. Kevin was so hungry for attention that he would easily consume every minute of my waking day if I let him. I was too immature at the time to realize how to set healthy boundaries with Kevin without destroying him in the process. Instead, I just became resentful of his continual presence, until eventually he caught on to my not-so-subtle hints of ignoring him. Understandably, he felt hurt. Eventually, he quit coming around altogether.

As outcast kids become involved and begin clamoring for our attention, it is easy to become resentful of their presence—to feel like spending time with them is not strategic to moving the group forward. One youth leader confided in me, "I'm not so concerned about how to get fringe kids here. I know they'll come. I'm much more concerned about the ramifications if they do start showing up."

2. They reveal our own personal prejudices. Much like the youth we deal with, we as adults also fear how associating with ostracized kids might stereotype us. After all, who wants a youth group full of nerds? Most of us would rather have our youth groups known as places where hip kids want to hang out.

Working with these kids can also remind us of our own feelings from adolescence. Perhaps we felt ostracized and alone at that age, too, and would prefer to keep those feelings well behind us. The fact that we are now accepted and adored by teenagers makes us feel good. Actively seeking out the shunned teenager brings back a lifetime of feelings of rejection and insecurity. Their mere presence becomes a constant reminder to us of how selfish and selective we really are in reaching out to others.

It is important for all of us to be willing to enter into honest self-examination. A good place to start is with the issue of obesity, so consistently an issue of ridicule and teasing.

• Are you repulsed by overweight people?

• When you first meet an overweight person, do you assume he or she is lacking in self-control?

• If you were interviewing an otherwise qualified candidate for a position, would you tend to not hire that person if he or she was overweight?

• Do you believe overweight people tend to be jolly and happy or sullen and morose?

• Do you see overweight people as fundamentally inferior?

If you answered yes to any of these questions, you need to recognize your prejudices. Repentance, prayer, and a new commitment to change are your only appropriate responses. God often uses fringe kids to reveal to us and heal us of our own sinful behavior.

A RADICAL APPROACH

While there are many barriers to reaching out to those who are unlike us and on the fringes of life, it is imperative that we do so. The strategy of targeting only those who are like us, or only the elite, has been extremely counterproductive for our youth groups. Not only is this nonbiblical and antithetical to Jesus' approach, it is responsible for many problems in our youth groups.

This strategy has contributed to the reality that we are not much different from every other adolescent social club. It is at least partially responsible for our teenagers being just as insecure and self-absorbed as those in the larger youth culture. Not only do fringe kids need youth groups, but youth groups also need fringe kids. Any youth group void of the marginalized kids of society is one that is likely lacking the power and mission of the Holy Spirit as well. It was Dietrich Bonhoeffer who so strongly warned, "The exclusion of the weak and insignificant, the seemingly useless people from a Christian community may actually mean the exclusion of Christ."[2]

Determining to reach beyond these barriers requires a radical strategy. Doing so may raise a few eyebrows, bring on the wrath of some, and backfire from time to time, but would Jesus do any less? His interaction with the outcast woman at the well in John 4 fills more space than any other individual encounter recorded in that Gospel. In fact, most of his recorded encounters were with lepers, demoniacs, and the disabled—all people shunned by both the religious folk and society in general.

Interestingly, it was around this very issue that Jesus was most heavily criticized. "He hangs around with prostitutes and sinners," they shouted. He was declared "a friend of tax collectors and sinners," a title that sounds much more appealing to us today than how it was originally intended.

Yet Jesus was completely uncompromising when it came to truth. He is our example. But because he was misunderstood, it is a pretty sure bet that we will be also. That does not excuse us from reaching out in love, however. To persist under such pressure requires a decision to persist, as well as a clear understanding of why it is not even an option for the serious Christian.

It is essential that we possess an understanding of Christ's call to value others as the image of God. Whenever Mother Teresa was asked why she spent so much time with the poor, she always responded, "I don't know any poor people, only images of Jesus."[3]

Perhaps the Jewish philosopher Martin Buber carried this thought the furthest of any modern thinker. He explained how significant our being created in God's image is because it teaches us that in connecting deeply with others, we are participating in our relationship with God. People are not objects, but possess intrinsic value in that they are created in God's image. As Buber explains, "God is present when I confront You. But if I look away from You, I ignore him. As long as I merely experience or use you, I deny God. But when I encounter You I encounter him."[4]

Not only are young people today able to comprehend such things, they are yearning to do so. We must be there to lead them by our words and actions.

SOMETIMES THE SMALLEST THINGS COUNT MOST

It is not our job to shoulder all of the responsibility for the kids we work with. Attempting to do so puts us in the place of God and eventually causes us to burn out. There are, however, some key things we can do, and even the smallest of them can make a tremendous difference.

JOHN

John has been a volunteer youth-group leader for many years. He has always spent much of his time with those so-called geeks and freaks—kids he meets during the daily routine of his life at malls, on street corners, and in restaurants where many of them work. He says he can relate to these kids because that's how he felt as a teenager.

John always figured that a youth group should be the safest place in the world for such kids, but he soon discovered that wasn't the case. The issues that keep such kids on the outside at school are the very same ones at work in the youth group. These obstacles are difficult to overcome, but not impossible.

John would bring fringe kids to youth group each week, sit with them, introduce them to other kids, and take them home afterwards. He didn't do this just at his own church, but at several others as well, because the kids he was meeting came from many different areas.

Eventually, the youth group kids got to know John's kids, and they all began to feel more comfortable with one another. Amazing things happened as these unlikely candidates became integrated into the mainstream of youth groups all over Massachusetts.

Recently John was reminiscing with me about four of those kids:

"My buddy Tim, our youth pastor, and I invited some of the outcast kids we had met to go skiing with us in New Hampshire. They said, 'Sure,' so we headed up with 'Bones,' a skateboarder with half a head of hair; Chris, his sidekick; Kevin, the class nerd in his school; and Tom, a smart but somewhat awkward overweight kid who faced daily harassment in school.

"We didn't do anything special aside from spending time and having fun with them. We did have a blast. We laughed, we skied, and we played cards. We even prayed at the end. That entire crew started coming to the youth group after that.

"That was in the mid-1980s. Two years ago, Kevin invited me to his wedding. He is in the military now and has a beautiful wife and child. Bones is now twenty-six, a college grad, and a friend. Chris is a successful businessman living on Martha's Vineyard. Tom graduated from Wheaton College and is working for a desktop publisher. He became quite popular at Wheaton, but he never turned it against those who were not.

"I'm sure that many factors went into helping those so-called outcasts make it through. But I like to think that a weekend on the slopes and one night a week for a couple of years helped them to realize just how special they were to God and to us."

the climate of our youth groups

The culture of cruelty that exists in most middle and secondary schools, as well as a large number of youth groups, simply must be confronted and changed. But change doesn't happen by simply making rules. As one teenager put it, "The only way to get kids not to hurt each other is to get kids not to want to hurt each other."[1] Attempting to create such a culture is what this chapter is all about.

Most of us attempt to deal with difficult situations by implementing policies designed to address those occasional serious matters of behavior that surface. For example, if a fight breaks out after youth group, a policy is created to no longer allow kids to hang out after youth group events. This is an unfortunate way to handle situations because it imposes negative consequences on everyone that are based on the isolated actions of a few.

It is far better to concentrate on establishing and maintaining a positive climate, rather than focusing on the occasional thunderstorm that emerges, as is illustrated below:

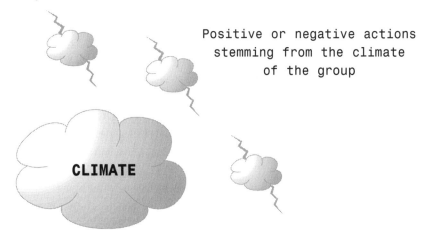

Positive or negative actions stemming from the climate of the group

CLIMATE

Unfortunately, this pattern of focusing on the occasional thunderstorm rules in a day and age when people are more motivated by fear than by logic. Banning trench coats, installing metal detectors, and hiring security guards in schools are all examples of attempting to influence the climate of a group through policies based upon occasional glitches instead of the other way around.

Several weeks after the Columbine school killings, I was teaching a group of youth ministry students from Philadelphia. One of the youth pastors in the class told about Matt, a boy in his youth group. When Matt's teacher asked how the class felt the Littleton massacre could have happened, Matt's words were carefully scrutinized by school officials. In fact, Matt was arrested that evening and held without bail, for fear that he might be plotting violence against his own classmates.

This pattern was repeated in communities across the country as school officials and politicians frantically rushed to establish policies addressing symptoms rather than core problems. In fact, most laws dealing with juveniles have been created and passed in the aftermath of such high-profile events. We are then forced to live with the negative long-term effects of poorly thought through policies. This chapter focuses on proactive methods that can be useful in developing loving and embracing climates.

DEVELOPING HEALTHY CLIMATES IN OUR YOUTH GROUPS

Youth groups can be wonderful training grounds for young people to learn how to respect one another and still have fun. Humor is a critical element in the lives of youth, but many have a hard time knowing when their humor goes too far. The fine line between healthy fun and destructive humor that depends on sacrificing the dignity of another can sometimes be blurry. Later in this chapter we will discuss how to help kids identify that critical boundary.

Youth groups can also be a place where kids learn to accept others unconditionally without necessarily condoning their actions. This is a particularly difficult concept for today's young person. The "new tolerance," as some have termed it, has a hard time separating one's actions from their personhood.

Historically, it has been acceptable to follow St. Augustine's charge to love the sinner while hating the sin. In our postmodern times, tolerance demands that we embrace both the individual and his or her lifestyle, regardless of how sinful it may be. Yet when someone crosses a certain line, as a culture we become completely intolerant, vehemently dispensing the most severe forms of punishment. For example, the United States is one of only six nations to execute minors or incarcerate fourteen-year-olds within the general population of adult prisons—both of which violate International Law. The other countries are Pakistan, Saudi Arabia, Iran, Nigeria, and Yemen.[2] Such tragedies are the fruits of a society that does not know how to love and care for sinners while hating and confronting their sinful behavior.

Biblically functioning youth groups have the opportunity to teach kids how to successfully live within these two tensions. When youth groups function as God intended, they are countercultural in every way. According to the dictionary we should all be *fringe* people, for the term is defined as "that which is outside or marginal to the mainstream."

Not only should the message we proclaim go against the grain of mainstream culture, but the climate we create should be just as revolutionary. The remainder of this chapter deals with how to develop such an environment.

THE IMPORTANCE OF CLIMATE

A long tradition of research has revealed that bullying differs much more by school than by state or region. This is because "the feel" or social climate of a group is what most influences the behavior of its members. For example, in schools with a more positive and predictable social climate, students learn measurably more. Where anti-bullying programs have been introduced in schools, there is less bullying and other anti-social behaviors such as vandalism, fighting, and truancy have been reduced. There is also a marked improvement in the positive climate of the school.[3]

In a Christian youth group, sacrificial love and acts of service are not only expected but are central to the Church's mission. As John 13:35 says, "Everyone will know that you are my disciples, if you have love for one another" (The New Revised Standard Version). A climate of genuine love is predictive of how successful we will be in attracting new members. It is also a very real indicator of the presence of Christ in our midst.

The social climate of the church youth group, and the entire church for that matter, is made up of the sum total of all the relationships between its members. Certain factors are strong indicators of a healthy climate.

• the degree to which new members feel comfortable

• old members' level of comfort in bringing new members into the fellowship

• the degree to which such actions are maintained by coercion versus being taught with a spirit of affection and cooperation

• the quality of adult-youth interactions

• the amount of teasing and taunting that takes place

• the amount of bullying or other coercive behaviors that occur when adults are not present

• the amount of tolerance for differences in appearance, dress, custom, language, or body type (so long as these differences do not place the mission of the church in jeopardy)

We have included a self-assessment questionnaire for both youth and adult leaders in Appendix 2 (p. 141) to help you evaluate your program's climate.

THE USE OF WORDS

Perhaps the biggest indicator of a group's climate is how members use words. While most young people understand how physical bullying destroys one's sense of security, many fail to recognize the destructive nature of verbal nastiness. In reality, many more are devastated by careless sarcasm, ridicule, and teasing than by physical acts of brutality.

The first step in dealing with unpleasant verbal behavior in a youth group is to establish clear expectations for what types of words will not be tolerated. This is especially important today since the style of humor prevalent on television and in movies that depends upon put-downs to generate laughter has infiltrated every corner of contemporary society.

Leaders should be able to articulate in a sentence or two the expectations for how people are to be treated during youth group activities. They should also be prepared to enforce these standards as well as to lead by example. Like all vision statements, this one should be no more than a sentence or two in length. The ramifications of the vision statement should be explainable in a paragraph or two. Having youth involved in the process of developing such a vision statement will make it far more effective, as well as ensure that it is actually practiced.

There are numerous biblical texts from which a vision statement can develop. The "new command" Jesus gave to "love one another...as I have loved you" (John 13:34) is a good place to start. Most important, though, is how the vision statement plays itself out from week to week. In the weekly Bible studies we conduct in over one hundred fifty juvenile jails, leaders explain the ground rules whenever there are several new faces:

1. Only one person speaks at a time.

2. Each person's opinion is respected.

3. No one speaks negatively about others—whether they are present or not.

These simple rules give kids both a sense of security and respect. They know that if they are absent one week no one will speak negatively about them behind their backs. It also allows us to respectfully confront kids who break the rules, not by attacking them, but by simply reminding them of our shared commitment to respect one another.

TEASING

When young people describe their experiences of being bullied, they are predominately verbal. And teasing is by far the most common type of verbal bullying by children of all ages.[4] Many perceive the verbal harassment they received as being just as threatening to their safety as physical attacks. So much for the old adage, "Sticks and stones may break my bones but words will never hurt me."

There seems to be a great deal of confusion for both youth and adults when it comes to teasing. For example, an overwhelming majority of teenagers believe that most teasing is "done in fun, not to hurt others." On the other hand, that same majority defined teasing as bullying and reported feeling traumatized by it.[5]

The confusion is understandable, for even the word "tease" has two completely divergent definitions. One is "to playfully fool around," while the other is "to annoy or harass by persistent mocking or poking fun."

During a focus panel John Hoover was conducting with a group of eleventh graders in a small Christian school, one young man confessed, "We tease each other a lot here, and sometimes I wonder if I may be hurting someone's feelings. I guess I'm not sure how to tell if I am."

As they brainstormed ways to deal with this issue, many positive ideas surfaced. One was to respectfully ask whether the teasing was becoming hurtful. Another was to watch for defensive body language or other signs that an individual might be disengaging from the group.

Just as the conversation was wrapping up, one young girl stood up and, in a loud but tremulous voice, said, "You guys have teased me about my weight since I was in the third grade. I hated it then and I hate it now!" As she was speaking, her classmates' faces expressed both shock and horror.

A young man was concerned enough to worry that he had been hurting others' feelings, but had never asked. A young woman had been hurting for seven years, but had never had the courage to share it with her classmates. Simply creating a context in which to discuss such things was able to bring resolution to years of hurt and confusion. How often do similar scenarios play themselves out around us?

Such hurts do not occur exclusively among our young people. Having served in leadership in a local church for many years, I try to meet with people who decide to leave in an effort to address legitimate concerns they may have had. Seldom is it over issues of music or message that they have become disgruntled. More often, it is the result of pain or grief inflicted by another parishioner's insensitive remarks. In most cases, I'm sure that the offender would not even recall having made the remarks, or certainly would not have intended such harm by them.

One would hope that we as Christians might speak more honestly with one another when offended or concerned about whether a statement we made might have hurt another. We can all learn from what that small band of kids in the Christian school focus group experienced. I'm always grateful when people have the guts to confront me about an off-handed comment I made or my lack of sensitivity. I realize that by doing so, they preserve our relationship from the resentment and bitterness that so easily festers when unattended.

FRAMES AND PHRASES

There are many characteristics of verbal exchanges that can predict whether something intended humorously will likely be misunderstood, such as the audience and the way the words are said. Being able to tell someone when they have hurt you and asking when in doubt about teasing are skills that must be learned. Unlike physical maturation, these skills do not develop naturally. The acquisition of social skills is similar to learning a language.

As adults, we sometimes forget how difficult it is to be a child and all the natural insecurity that goes along with that phase of life. Add to that the fact that most people, adults included, do not know how to appropriately express their feelings of hurt.

Young people crave the help and guidance of adults when it comes to deciphering appropriate and inappropriate verbal behavior. Most want help and support in learning social skills which will aid them in their lives. While schoolyards can be dangerous places for youngsters to practice new techniques of openness and vulnerability, youth groups should not be. One of the most helpful methods to teach such skills to youth group kids is through the use of *frames and phrases*.[6]

Frames

Using the analogy of a picture frame can be helpful to illustrate to kids how teasing can cross the line into bullying. Through this tangible comparison, young people are able to visualize how humor that starts out harmlessly can end disastrously.

Picture two people residing together within the borders of a frame. Their relationship is secure enough to handle verbal interchanges even when they may appear to carry a nasty edge. This is because each knows that the other has an unswerving commitment to their relationship that transcends the use of words. They have learned to communicate effectively with each other. There is mutual trust and respect. They have learned to speak the truth in love. Teasing can be received in a spirit of good humor because of the assurance that it was given that way.

However, when one party feels outside the frame, because of any number of real or perceived barriers, confusion and hurt feelings can easily result. While a comment may not have been intended for hurt, the recipient is not sure what hidden feelings might exist behind the remark. Because the individuals do not reside within the same border, the relationship may not be able to withstand teasing. In that case, either parties should refrain from teasing or efforts should be made to ensure that both parties are within the same border before teasing is done.

There are many situations that make it difficult for two people to exist within the same frame. A partial list is provided below. It is important to teach young people this list and encourage them to think before they tease. Use the list to help other students recognize when their teasing may have crossed the line into bullying, or is in danger of doing so.

1. DIFFERENT GENDERS – On many topics, girls and boys will be out of one another's frame and therefore should refrain from teasing unless they are confident that their relationship can handle it. Comments about clothes, body type, or facial appearance are particularly sensitive across gender lines.

2. RACIAL AND ETHNIC BOUNDARIES – Given the history of racial relationships in North America, it is difficult to joke across racial and ethnic lines. Words that can be spoken freely and humorously within racial groups carry an offensive edge when delivered by an outsider. This doesn't mean that deep and solid friendships cannot be fostered across the lines. However, special care must be taken to prevent inappropriate types of teasing.

3. AUDIENCE – Borders can shift based on who is present. Jimmy may be able to tease Alex in good humor within their circle of good friends. But if he makes the same remark before a different audience, such as fourth period math class, Alex is suddenly outside the border. Now it appears as though Jimmy is attempting to gain the acceptance of others at Alex's expense. Such actions produce hard feelings and resentment that can take years to overcome.

4. PERSONALITY ISSUES – Because of differences in personality, thinking, and language skills, some youngsters do not readily "get" sarcasm or irony. They will not appreciate teasing because they don't understand the affectionate humor underlying the rather tough-sounding words. Some of these youngsters have a history of physical or emotional abuse associated with verbal humor and have become thin-skinned about any kind of humor or teasing that comes at their expense.

5. HAVING A BAD DAY – One day a person can handle teasing without a problem. But on another, even words delivered in good faith from good friends in ideal surroundings inflict hurt and pain. Being tired, sick, or just having a bad day shrinks the borders of a person's picture frame. Thus, the friend who resided within your borders yesterday may be outside of them today, due to no fault of him or you. Such realities require sensitivity on the part of those who might otherwise be able to tease in healthy ways.

For example, John Hoover recalls being informed during an early morning visit with his physician that he needed to lose some weight. Later that afternoon, when a group of friends jokingly kidded him about eating a cookie, he reacted much more strongly to the good-natured ribbing than he might otherwise. The dimensions of his borders had shifted, at least in reference to that particular topic.

Phrases

Not only is the context within which teasing occurs critical, but the way in which words are delivered is also crucial. Below are some guidelines that can help young people discern the difference between healthy teasing and destructive bullying.

1. Avoid teasing anybody about physical characteristics.

2. Use humor about yourself and some of the foolish things you do more often than you call attention to others' quirks.

3. Never tease people about things you suspect they may be sensitive about.

4. Never use humor or teasing as a way to get back at people or to make a point about something you're unwilling to confront them directly on.

5. Avoid calling anybody a name that you wouldn't want to be called. Others pick up quickly on names like "Fatso," "Waddles," or "Stringbean," and these names tend to stick.

6. Never make degrading comparisons of people to detestable objects such as excrement or to an animal such as a cow or a dog.

7. Never say things publicly that you learned in private, thereby breaking confidence and confidentiality.

Intervening With Appropriate Phrases

Another way phrases can be used effectively is to share our own problem-solving approaches with young people. This is a very effective means of teaching helpful principles, as our input tends to be seen as less of an attack and more as advice from a fellow traveler.

Below are some examples of such phrases:

1. "Sometimes I wonder if in joking with friends I might actually be insulting them."

2. "When I worry that I may have insulted someone, I feel better when I've asked them about it. It helps to put the issue behind us."

3. "Sometimes my feelings are hurt when people say unkind things to me. I think that's pretty normal."

4. "More often than not, I find it very helpful to let people know how I feel."

5. "If someone persists in insulting me in front of others, I try to avoid them if I can. If that doesn't work, I might try to get someone to mediate between us."

6. "I would be hurt if someone I didn't know well teased me about the way I look, especially in front of other people."

Think of some phrases that you use, and add them to the list. Make them as specific as possible. When you share them with young people, add actual examples. Tell about times the phrases worked or times you failed to apply them and the negative consequences that resulted.

The More Direct Approach

Once kids see that we struggle with many of the same issues they do, they are more willing to grant us permission to speak more directly to them. You might want to counsel individuals by using some of the following phrases:

1. "Perhaps that's a topic Joan doesn't like to talk about, or maybe she's having a bad day."

2. "Even if you meant it in fun, it may have hurt Jenny's feelings. That could be something she is sensitive about."

3. "Boys often say things like that to break the ice when they can't think of anything else to say."

4. "When someone says something that I don't like, I tell them in a firm but not aggressive way that I don't like it. Let's think together about what you might say to Sally."

5. "It does hurt when people bring that topic up. Sometimes my friends tease me about things I don't like, too. But after I calm down, I usually realize that it's a good idea to talk to them about it."

6. "Occasionally, African-American students might say things to each other that are inappropriate for European-Americans to say. It probably has nothing to do with you personally, but when you say it, you might inflict pain just because you are of a different race."

7. "Sometimes I say something I thought was funny, but it turns out to hurt another person. Then I usually think to myself, 'Maybe it wasn't the right time or place, or maybe they were having a bad day.' Is that possibly what happened in this case? Do you think maybe you should apologize?"

8. "People are almost always offended if you tease them about something they're sensitive about, especially in front of others. How do you think what you said might have felt to her?"

Problem Solving

The last use for phrases is in teaching kids a step-by-step approach to deal with teasing or other types of bullying. Youngsters can be taught to WAIT, CONSIDER, DECIDE, READ, and ASK. Below is a list of principles they can be taught:

1. WAIT: Is the statement I'm about to make one that could be easily misunderstood?

2. CONSIDER: Considering all I have been taught about the role of race issues, gender, sensitive topics, and situations, I need to ask myself: "Am I comparing a person to an object or an animal?" "Is this an embarrassing time or place to tease her about this?" and so on.

3. DECIDE: If the situation is likely to end with hard feelings, Jesus would want me to hold my tongue, so I will.

4. READ: Even if I tease people in a good-natured way, does their body language or facial appearance tell me they may have misunderstood my intentions?

5. ASK: If the answer to number four is yes, ask them about it privately.

If they confirm that the teasing bothers them or their body language says so, apologize and stop doing it.

The key to making this method work is to help students remember and practice the process. Use of catchy memory devices can be helpful. For example, the above process might be more easily remembered through the use of the silly phrase, "I am going to Waco, dear." In other words I am going to WAit, COnsider, DEcide, Ask, and Read before I verbally joke with someone. Having students develop a role-play or skit for each of these steps or illustrate them through a poster or collage cements the learning for them that much more.

Some of this may seem rather petty and insignificant, but in the months following several of the school tragedies, students gathered to reflect on what they had learned and how they could prevent it from reoccurring. One freshman at Columbine High School said, "I don't tease my friends as much as I used to. I try to be a lot nicer now to everybody." Another explained, "A lot of us [seniors] have been more open to people, even underclassmen...I just think that's a huge responsibility for us."[7]

Of course, it is best to develop preventative measures rather than having to react after the fact. The most effective strategies are those devised by young people themselves rather than adult-generated ones. Once youth groups are involved in developing preventative measures, have them create clever ways to remember and practice them. Discuss with them what sort of consequences ought to be enforced and how violators should be handled. This ensures that the entire group participates in the process, not just the adults.

For example, one youth group decided that first or second violators of their covenant would receive a gentle, loving admonition from one of their fellow students, informing them of their commitment to create an environment where everyone feels supported and built up. Subsequent violations would result in having the violator meet with the person offended and one adult leader. The youth group has never had to resort to the second consequence.

The positive effects of such a process were recently seen in our own youth group. Ginny received the following note a couple of days after inviting her thirteen-year-old friend Justin to attend the group.

> *Your youth group is great! It's fun and it helped me get more in touch with God. I never really was involved in religion before, but I felt very comfortable. It's the only place I've ever been where everyone is popular. Thanks for taking me. Now, I realize what a true friend you are.*

When I inquired further about Justin, Ginny explained, "This was his first time at any youth group meeting so he was a little nervous. He doesn't really have any friends at school. Kids think he's gay because of how he dresses."

Some kids wear WWJD bracelets to school. Others, like Ginny, just do it.

risk
IN OUR MIDST

how to reach them

adults in the lives of kids

"I don't want to be reached. I don't want to be loved!" declared seventeen-year-old Ziggy. When asked why he felt that way he said, " 'Cause when I needed it, nobody was there. Do you hear me? Nobody was there! So I don't want it now." Kids like Ziggy are very difficult to connect with, and sadly, they are becoming more and more prevalent in our society.

Though historically the lives of children and adults were closely intertwined, ours may be the first culture where kids and grown-ups actually try hard to avoid one another. Not only do the lives of young and old rarely intersect, but the nature of their relationships has changed as well.

In the past, most teenagers tended to respect adults, but things have changed. Many of today's adults are actually afraid of young people. Youth researcher Peter Benson notes that 80 percent of adults actually avert their eyes when meeting youth of middle school age.

Perhaps one of the reasons we are so intimidated by teenagers is that our entire culture seems to revolve around them. They are the ones who know and embody all that is in style when it comes to clothing, music, and vocabulary. We adults are seen as "old-fashioned" and "out of touch."

One of the unfortunate results of this disconnection is that adults are no longer in a position to provide kids with the role models, security, and structure that they so desperately need. In many ways, it is the tragic fulfillment of the prophet Isaiah's words some twenty-six hundred years ago, "I will make boys their officials; mere children will govern them. The young will rise up against the old" (Isaiah 3:4-5b).

The following story illustrates what can happen when a child grows up without caring adults.

PAUL

Paul was born into a family where abuse and neglect had ruled for three generations. While his mother loved him deeply, she lacked the parenting skills and support system necessary to raise him.

Soon after she became pregnant with Paul, her husband, plagued with alcohol problems and the ghosts of Vietnam, hung himself. Born a few months later, Paul, Jr., was named in memory of his deceased dad.

During the time they resided in a stable Midwestern town, neighbors mostly shunned them. Even the Lutheran church, the primary social institution in the community, was not a welcoming environment for this young troubled family, though they attended several times. Isolated and unsupported, Paul's mother regularly battled depression and often neglected Paul and his older sister, LaRean.

Fortunately, the school principal took a keen interest in both children and they thrived there. Paul's second-grade teacher commented that he was never a discipline problem but was always eager to please, doing anything it took to get hugs and good grades.

In search of better employment, Mother moved the family to a neighboring community. Things didn't go nearly so well there. Harassed by peers and lacking supportive adults, LaRean responded aggressively when kids called her a slut, but Paul refused to fight. Instead he would run to his home in the trailer park, just ahead of his tormentors who shouted, "Go cry to your dead daddy!"

By fifth grade, Paul weighed two hundred pounds and was regularly mocked with cruel and vulgar names. He was very unhappy and seldom slept through the night. At age eleven, Paul was arrested for the first time on a charge of stealing beef jerky from a convenience store. Sentenced to four hours of community service at the city park, court records show that he willingly fulfilled his service and even went back the next day to ask the groundskeeper if he could work for free for the rest of the summer. Strangely enough, his request was denied.

A critical turning point in Paul's life came in the fifth grade when kids chased him home from school, throwing rocks at him. He locked himself in his trailer sobbing and believing there was nobody in the world who cared for him. By nightfall, he had decided to hang himself with a rope like his dad had done, fantasizing that he would go to heaven to be united with the father he never knew. As he twisted the rope tightly around his neck, he started to cry at the thought of how much this would hurt his sister. He decided that he couldn't kill himself, and that she was right: He had to learn to fight.

Larger than his peers, Paul quickly graduated from scapegoat to bully. He started hanging out with negative peers, roughhousing with them at recess, intimidating other kids on the way to school, and causing trouble in the classroom. As a result, he failed sixth grade twice, mostly because of his rare attendance.

Because of his truancy, twelve-year-old Paul was placed in a short-term residential treatment center. In those four months, Paul flourished. He loved the teachers and staff and threw himself into his studies. He even received the highest grades in the school. But soon he was discharged and back on the streets for the summer.

In the meantime, Paul's sister LaRean had found a new boyfriend named Shawn. Paul finally found the male role model he had been seeking for so long in Shawn. "He became like a father to me," beamed Paul.

But seventeen-year-old Shawn was mentoring Paul in delinquency. Desperate for approval, Paul began participating in minor thefts. Shawn would call him names like "lard-ass" and "sissy" whenever he balked. Their final act together would change Paul's life forever.

It was a taxicab robbery that was botched from the start. Once Shawn figured out that their voices were being taped through the cab's two-way radio, he began shouting self-serving things like, "What are you doing, Paul?" In the scuffle that followed, the driver was fatally shot.

Apprehended within minutes, Shawn explained to the police that he thought they were just going to a keg party when all of a sudden Paul took out a gun and robbed and shot the driver. Paul said nothing except to ask the police to take care of the driver's puppy that was left in the cab so it would not freeze to death.

Shawn received a reduced prison sentence in exchange for damaging testimony against Paul. Paul became the first fourteen-year-old in his state to be tried as an adult and given a life sentence without the possibility of parole.

Today, Paul's church is inside the walls of a prison. The chaplain says that Paul has a spiritual depth and hunger seldom seen in adults. Ironically, the prison chaplain had been the pastor of that little Lutheran church where Paul and his family first lived. He wrestles with the question of why neither he nor anybody else in that community reached out to the young widow and her small children, and how if they had, the story might have ended differently.[1]

DISCONNECTED FROM THE WORLD OF ADULTS

Paul's story is a tragic illustration of a child disconnected from adults. All his life he tried desperately to reach out to whoever might embrace him: neighbors, teachers, social workers, church folk, even the police. But in the end, it was only seventeen-year-old Shawn who paid him consistent attention.

Stories like Paul's are becoming more and more common in our day, but such stories weren't created over night. Much of our present-day crisis can be traced back more than one hundred years to when adolescence, as a term and concept, was first invented. Prior to the industrial revolution, the transition from childhood to adulthood was much smoother, as young people were more naturally apprenticed into the world of adulthood.

With the dawn of industrialization, youngsters became increasingly segregated from the world of adults. Work was removed from the home, and child labor laws were passed in response to the abuse of children in "sweat factories." While these laws were a necessary step to prevent the exploitation of children, the unforeseen consequence was the segregation of youth from adults and from the work force entirely. This gave youth large amounts of leisure time with one another and no real sense of purpose or responsibility.

During this same time, children were being placed in formalized schools where they were segregated into age-specific groups. As a result, adults began assuming much more "professional roles" in the lives of kids, such as teachers or counselors, instead of the more natural interactions they had enjoyed in a more rural culture.

By the 1940s, a host of other institutions were launched that even further segregated youth and adults. The scouting movement, age-graded high schools, and organized sports were all created with the sole purpose of socializing youth, a process that had always occurred much more naturally in earlier generations and continues still in more tribal communities.[2]

Most of the large parachurch youth organizations in existence today were birthed during this time, along with the invention of the youth pastor. All of these focused on this emerging subculture of society called adolescence. Now, rather than having a needed role or mission in society, youth became the new mission field, as great numbers of adults became trained to "reach them."

With this more professionalized approach to interacting with kids, less and less meaningful time was actually being spent with them. As a result, more and more young people are growing up with scarcely any quality contact with adults. Authors of the book *Being Adolescent: Conflict and Growth in the Teenage Years* Mihaly Csikszentmihalyi and Reed Larson found that teenagers spend only about 4.8 percent of their time with parents and only 2 percent with adults who are not their parents.[3] And those percentages keep shrinking.

While there is a tremendous emphasis on the needs of adolescents as a group these days, few seem to be paying much attention to the individuals who make up that group. When youth lack significant adult attachments, it is not hard to understand why they turn to the media for direction and nurture, devise their own alternative rites of passage into adulthood, and embrace substitute forms of spirituality.

NURTURED BY THE MEDIA

In the absence of significant adults to pass on values of faith and morality, the entertainment industry is eager to provide the road maps for kids. As a result, the relationship between the media and young people has become very symbiotic. Not only does the media depend on the billions of dollars young people spend on entertainment and advertised products, but youth also need the media to provide them with nurturing and guidance.

Sixteen-year-old Dustin described his attachment to music:

> *If you relate to these people, the music they sing will have a greater effect on you. I have listened to their music for the last few years and it seems like they are singing about me and the situations in my life. I know a lot of kids who use music as a counselor or therapist. Some music has a negative effect, like songs about killing your mom, killing your dad, killing God, and eventually killing yourself. But some songs are about how to make it through life even if you were dealt a bad hand.*
>
> *My favorite musician is Jonathan Davis who is lead singer in the band known as koRn. As a young kid he grew up abused and neglected and is now trying to make something out of his life. These people affect my life a lot. They show me that even though I didn't grow up the best way, I can still make my life into something.*

Other popular artists like Marilyn Manson, an outcast and bullied teenager even at the youth groups he occasionally attended as a kid, now call youth to fight back through hatred and revenge.[4] Anarchy and hedonism can become the highest aspiration for those who have never found love and acceptance.

Not only do kids relate to musicians, but many latch onto and live their lives out through the fantasies they see on the screen as well. Twelve-year-old Samantha explains how she can relate to "Monica," a neat-freak on the TV program *Friends*: "If you like a show, you take the actors on as role models."[5]

Today's young people are the first truly multimedia generation in the history of the world. From Mr. Rogers to MTV to the Internet, they have never known life apart from an ever-present media. As a result, many have developed an unusual bond with it. *Sesame Street* and *Arthur* are the most popular baby-sitters in our day and age. Their services are called upon many times each day as the average preschooler in America watches twenty-seven hours of television per week.[6]

As a result, countless children form attachments to characters like Barney, who become one of their primary teachers, and one through whom they learn and experience much of life. Research has shown that the average child actually gets more one-on-one attention from TV than from parents and teachers combined.[7]

This attachment continues into the teenage years, making it quite natural for young people to turn to talk show hosts, such as Jerry Springer, and sitcoms to educate them about life. As a result, they are exposed to a twisted version of real life. In fact, psychologists agree that before age ten, it is difficult for children to distinguish reality from the fantasy they observe on the screen.

ALTERNATIVE RITES OF PASSAGE

Traditionally, young people have learned adult roles through observing, imitating and interacting with the grown-ups around them. Such rituals of initiation as the Jewish bar mitzvah and bat mitzvah are very important rite-of-passage ceremonies for boys and girls turning thirteen years old. Many churches confer baptism, confirmation, or catechism as rites of passage to adulthood. Unfortunately, most of these rituals have come to represent little more than a party with some cash and gifts thrown in.

Membership initiation rituals into gangs are much more clear and concrete. Perhaps that is why gang memberships are growing at such high rates. When positive rituals and rites of passage into adulthood lose their place in society, teenagers tend to construct their own. "The first time I got wasted," "my first joint," or "the night I lost my virginity" take on significance for a young person who lacks positive benchmarks into adulthood. How else does one explain the fact that, despite tremendous public pressure and obvious health risks, teenagers continue to be the only age group in which cigarette smoking is on the increase?

Of course, negative rites of passage are mere counterfeits for the real thing. In the New Testament, the Greek word *koinonea* is translated "fellowship." It means to give, contribute, share; to be initiated into the mysteries of Christ; to participate in the deeds of others, being equally responsible for them.[8]

Embodied in this term *koinonea* is the basic definition of a gang, or at least what many perceive a gang is supposed to be. Yet, notice how *koinonea* functioned in the early church:

"All the believers were together and had everything in common. Selling their possessions and goods, they gave to anyone as he had need. Every day they continued to meet together in the temple courts. They broke bread in their homes and ate together with glad and sincere hearts, praising God and enjoying the favor of all the people. And the Lord added to their number daily those who were being saved" (Acts 2:44-47). I once read this to a group of gang members in a juvenile jail. The leader responded, "Where's that church? I'll join it."

The degree to which youth groups and churches are able to create true *koinonea* is the degree to which they will be effective in reaching those on the fringes of life.

SUBSTITUTE SPIRITUALITY

Throughout history, most societies have held spiritual truths in high esteem, ensuring that they are passed on from generation to generation. But as educators and child-care workers attempted to be more scientific in the twentieth century, moral and spiritual issues were pushed aside. The result was a century-long social experiment in operating a secular society cut adrift from its spiritual moorings.

As we enter a new century, however, modernism with its rationalistic approach is dead. Postmoderns are highly intrigued with the supernatural and spiritual dimensions. For example, Wicca, or white witchcraft, is one of the fastest growing religions today, especially among teenage girls. Likewise, one of the hottest crazes recently has been the *Harry Potter* children's book series, which chronicles the adventures of a young wizard whose parents were murdered and who now attends the Hogwarts School of Witchcraft and Wizardry.

While the vast majority of young people still hold to a belief in God, for the most part it is not the God of the Bible. Their theology is more influenced by television, movies, and books like *Harry Potter*. A friend recently told me of his visit to a local gift shop to purchase a necklace with a cross. The teenage girl waiting on him asked, "Do you want a plain cross or one with a little man on it?" It sounds absurd, but think about it. Who in today's culture is educating teenagers about who the "little man" is?

The dilemma facing the children of Israel after the death of Joshua rings just as true today: "After that whole generation had been gathered to their fathers, another generation grew up, who knew neither the Lord nor what he had done for Israel. Then the Israelites did evil in the eyes of the Lord and served the Baals" (Judges 2:10-11).

As Christians we may be tempted to grasp for simplistic answers like putting prayer back in schools or posting the Ten Commandments in classrooms, but it is naive to think that with the mere enforcement of external standards we can alter the inner life of teenagers and somehow usher them back to a more innocent time. Today's youth are worlds apart from those of even a generation prior. The strategy to reach them must be as radical as the problem itself.

WHAT KIDS NEED FROM ADULTS

I met Traci at a youth retreat. She was obviously overstressed in a number of areas of her life, a common characteristic of so many young people today. At the end of our conversation, I asked her if she had shared any of this with her parents. She answered, "No, they already have enough problems of their own. They don't have time for my problems too."

Most teenagers who have succumbed to irrational or violent behavior say they felt like the world was just caving in on them, like there was no way out. Tragically, it is at this very point that the majority of our young people feel they have no adults to talk to. Obviously, relationships with adults must be forged before the point of crisis for a teenager to feel that he or she has an adult ally who can be trusted.

Even the kids we think are most incurable long for guidance. They want to be heard and, at some level, stopped from doing destructive things. As one youngster told me, "I just want someone to care enough to tell me, 'No.' "

One major study revealed that while kids do go to each other first for advice, they tend not to trust the advice they receive. The overwhelming response of youth surveyed was that they would prefer to go to their parents or other adults first, but youth do not believe they have a relationship with parents or adults that allows them to talk openly about their problems.[9]

When kids become overwhelmed with the problems in their lives, they need others who can help give them perspective—people who can help them work through their problems and assure them that "this too will pass." In the absence of such relationships, kids have only peers with whom to process their confusion. But often, peers only serve to escalate a young person's feelings of distress. Rarely are they able to offer a voice of wisdom and balanced perspective that comes with having *been there*. This is when the listening ear of a caring adult trusted by a young person is so critically important.

A SENSE OF IDENTITY

One of the most important things kids receive from healthy adults is a sense of what it means to be a man or a woman. Girls need women to teach and model what it means to be a healthy woman. The media cannot confer that. Peers can't provide it. It takes a healthy adult woman to provide that.

Likewise, boys need healthy men to teach them what it means to be a man. While mothers do many essential things, one thing they cannot do is model for a boy how to be a man. In a Los Angeles Times Magazine cover story entitled "Mothers, Sons, and the Gangs," each of the several single mothers lamented, "I don't understand why my boy hangs out on the streets. I'm a good mother. I keep a clean house. I go to church. I don't run around with men. I cook for the boy, wash his clothes, and provide a good home. Why doesn't he want to stay here?"[10]

How does a boy learn what it means to be a man? Robert Bly explains it this way:

"When a father and son do spend long hours together...we could say that a substance almost like food passes from the older body to the younger. The son's body—not his mind—receives and the father gives this food at a level far below consciousness. His cells receive some knowledge of what an adult masculine body is. The younger body learns at what frequency the masculine body vibrates. It begins to grasp the song that adult male cells sing."[11]

Research has clearly shown that when a good father influence is missing, boys lack a healthy understanding of what male identity is. So they tend to act out very exaggerated notions of masculinity, including extreme aggression, sexual promiscuity, and physical abuse of women.[12]

Of course, a mother's role is no less critical than that of a father. Of the thirty boys who have lived with us after coming out of jail, three had been abandoned by their mothers. They were far more damaged and maladjusted than any of the others, even those growing up without a father.

Maternal care and affection, especially in the early years of a child's life, are critical for that youngster to be able to form significant bonding relationships later in life.[13] A second detrimental effect of growing up without a healthy mother is often revealed in a young person's lack of good communication skills. Researchers say that mothers generally have more influence than fathers on the way children come to think and behave in relating to others.[14]

In both sons and daughters, mothers tend to provide a sense of security, while a father's influence instills a healthy sense of self-confidence.[15] Whenever young people are reared without healthy mothers or fathers, it is absolutely essential that other adults come alongside and invest in them.

DEVELOPMENTAL ISSUES

The role adults play in the lives of such kids is key, but children need different things from adults at different stages in their development, as in the following chart.

Bonds Between Children and Adults		
STAGE OF DEVELOPMENT	MOST IMPORTANT NEED	ADULT ROLE
INFANT/TODDLER	•my needs	•satisfy needs
PRESCHOOL	•please adults	•teach standards •provide approval
ELEMENTARY	•be fair	•uphold authority •guide behavior
MIDDLE SCHOOL	•fit in •gain respect	•model •facilitate interactions
HIGH SCHOOL	•do what's right •care for others	•advocate •be a confidant

Adapted from material from Mary Wood, Developmental Therapy and Teaching Institute, Athens, GA.

We know that whenever abuse, trauma, or heavy drug and alcohol use invades the life of a young person, emotional development comes to a halt.[16] Kids tend to remain stuck there emotionally, though their bodies continue developing. Thus, many troubled high school students are still dealing with issues that should have been healthily resolved earlier in life. As a result, issues of fairness, power, and respect, which are normally resolved in middle school, are still enormous for many troubled high school teenagers. Sometimes their unmet needs are even more elementary, such as seeking to please adults or having assurance that one's basic needs will be met.

If one examines today's prison environment, it remarkably parallels the culture of a middle school where issues of respect, power, and pecking order abound. Middle school has always been a brutal place as kids seek to work through these issues. When ninety-five-pound kids struggle to figure out the pecking order on playgrounds, the result is a few bloody noses and an occasional black eye. But when such issues are still being worked out in adults with two-hundred-pound bodies, or with those who have easy access to weapons, the results are much more tragic. There is no jungle quite like that of grown-ups living in a middle school world.

Healthy adults are absolutely essential for young people to resolve these developmental issues. When this does not happen in middle school, it needs to happen in high school or beyond.

A HIGH RISK FACTOR—BEING MALE

As we already mentioned, one of the highest risk factors present in teenagers who become violent is simply *being male.* In fact, boys and men commit 90 percent of the violence in our culture.[17] While bullying is a problem for both boys and girls, why is it only boys who have lashed out in such violent and heinous ways?

Much of it comes down to this issue of male identity. So much of the media's portrayal of manhood portrays violence as the language of real men. Consider the current multimillion-dollar World Wrestling Federation (WWF) craze. Though most of it is staged and fake, this so-called sport still promotes blood thirstiness like that of the gladiators in first-century Rome.

Even more disturbing are popular video games like *Doom* and *Quake,* marketed primarily to boys, that promote brutal vengeance as a means of dealing with obstacles. They allow already-enraged boys to practice extremely brutal acts, with no sense of reality or consequence for such behavior. In videotapes shot just before the Columbine killings Eric Harris said, "It's going to be like *Doom.* Tick, tick, tick, tick...Haa! That shotgun is straight out of *Doom!*"[18]

All boys need to learn healthy ways to deal with the critical issues of empowerment and respect if they are to develop a healthy male identity. When denied these, they are left seething with rage.

Empowerment

Empowerment has always been a primary issue in the lives of teenagers. By empowerment, we mean possessing a measure of control over what happens in one's life, having a voice in decisions, being asked for opinions and ideas. It is part of a natural maturation process all adolescents must go through to enter healthy adulthood.

When we deny kids healthy empowerment they often respond in one of two ways. Either they become so insecure and incompetent that they are afraid to make decisions on their own or they rebel against everything their parents stand for.

Therefore, rather than getting into power struggles with kids at youth group, look for ways to empower them by giving them significant tasks and responsibilities. Rather than exerting control over them, place yourself under them where appropriate, so that you need their help to accomplish the goals of the youth group.

I often seek out those kids who cause the most problems and tell them how much I need them if I'm going to get through to their friends or maintain control in the youth group. "They'll listen to you more than me," I say. "Can you help me by getting them to be quiet and attentive during our meetings?"

"Sure, no problem," they usually respond. "I'll take care of them."

The fact that they feel needed will bring them out to church and youth group events more than anything else. And in most cases they rise to, and beyond, our level of expectation.

Respect

As adults, we often lament the fact that teenagers don't show us the respect we deserve. While some of that is just part of being adolescent, some of it also stems from the reality that most of us don't tend to show them much respect either.

John Hoover recalls an argument he had with his parents about music when he was thirteen years old. In the midst of it his father adamantly declared that the Beatles were "lousy" and their popularity "would never last." That was the first time John began consciously questioning his parents' perfection.

It is natural for teenagers to leave many of their parents' values temporarily behind, forming a generational loyalty to one another. This is part of the normal individuation process. Thus, when adults challenge the ideas and ideals of youth too quickly, they alienate themselves from them all the more. Just as John understood how naive and misinformed his parents were about music, kids disregard us when they recognize our ignorance as well.

Showing a respectful interest in the music and media of teenagers is one way to show appreciation and respect for their developing identities. This does not mean we must approve of their every interest, but the criticism can wait for the relationship to develop.

One of the most effective youth workers at Hoover's home church was Mrs. Towne. She passionately communicated with young people about music and movies. Her stance was always one of respect, even when she disapproved of some of the choices the youngsters made. Because kids recognized she was well informed, and because of how she engaged them in the discussions, they were much more open to her input and often heeded what she had to say.

This issue of respect is at the core of much of today's teenage violence. Michael Carneal, the boy who murdered three classmates in Kentucky, said what he really wanted more than anything else was "respect from the kids."[19]

Many troubled youth come to believe that protecting that thin layer of self-respect can be more important than even preserving their own lives. When a troubled young person loses this self-respect, he is in a dangerous predicament. There is a fine line between violence against others and self-destruction in such youth. One young person who was locked up for plotting a massacre of his tormentors said, "If I could have killed a dozen of them, it would have been worth giving up my own life."

Bullied kids often feel that they are forced to strike out first. Most carry tremendous amounts of anger within them, causing them to show either no emotion or mostly negative emotions. One young man confessed, "The reason I don't like myself is because I'm a nobody. I'm not an athlete. I'm not smart. I don't have any friends. In fact, the only thing that keeps me going is that I hate other people more than I hate myself."

Thus, it is imperative that when we confront such kids, it be done respectfully. Always avoid confrontation in front of their peers where they may be embarrassed or humiliated. Instead, take them aside and say something like, "You know, you have really become a significant part of our youth group program and I value your presence here a great deal. It's because of how much I appreciate you and how committed I am to you that I feel we need to talk about some things…" Not only will they appreciate your respect, but the fact that you care enough to confront them will speak volumes.

creating fringe-kid friendly environments

Peer influence becomes potent the moment children enter school. As they move towards adolescence, normal children become steadily more responsive to classmates and less dependent on adults. But many youth who are ostracized by peers actually relate much better with adults than with one another.

Part of this comes from the tendency of bullied kids to become overly enmeshed in unhealthy family relationships, while lacking the skills to relate well with others their age. In other words, they identify so closely with the dysfunctional family unit that they have difficulty functioning with those outside their home. Such children feel more comfortable with adults but feel threatened in unsupervised activities with other children. Their trepidation not only undercuts their ability to deal with others their age, but it also attracts the attacks of bullies.

In addition, the interests of bullied children are often more compatible with adult interests than with those of classmates. As a result, many of them are much more invested in higher-demand intellectual exercises than are others their age. More in-depth Bible study may prove very appealing to them.

John Hoover interviewed one young man named Eric who had suffered greatly at the hands of his grade school and middle school classmates. Yet in high school, Eric reported being happy and grateful that he was no longer being bullied.

When asked what happened, he shrugged and said, "When I got to high school, there were other computer nerds like me. And I made friends in the chess club." During these years, an older mentor also helped him become a computer expert. Part of the reason he did so well in high school was the fact that he had mastered a skill and could now assist others who needed help with math and computer assignments. Helping needy peers helped Eric develop a stronger sense of meaning and purpose.

Not all such youngsters fare as well as Eric. Though some may appear quite mature, looks can be deceiving. An intellectually advanced child may be severely stunted socially or emotionally. Both areas require significant interaction with healthy adults and peers to develop properly. Thus, isolation from kids their own age does not help them in the end.

THREE DAMAGING SCENARIOS

The problem with so many children growing up in our culture is that they lack both healthy adult relationships and healthy peer relationships. Such youngsters are susceptible to three potentially damaging scenarios.

First, they may become loners who feel like they don't fit in anywhere. As one young man so pointedly said, "To be an outcast is to be a 'nonperson,' " Second, they may bond to negative peers who will offer acceptance. Children who lack positive relationships with adults are prone to form destructive connections as they seek peers with similar problems. Luke Woodham, the sixteen-year-old who murdered three students in Pearl, Mississippi, told ABC News that he felt isolated and rejected in his community. Thus, he was easily drawn into a group of boys who were self-proclaimed Satanists. The third damaging scenario takes place when such kids become prey for unhealthy adults with ulterior motives. Dangerous cults and groups that profit from the sexual exploitation of children actively recruit young outcasts because they know how easily they can be enticed.

Kids in all three scenarios are at great risk of inflicting harm on themselves or others. Void of healthy outside perspectives, their world becomes wrapped in the pain of the present. Unable to visualize how things could possibly change for the better, they feel trapped and hopeless. Anyone who falls into that sort of hopelessness is in a dangerous predicament.

YOUTH GROUPS FULFILLING THEIR CALLING

While today's generation of young people exhibit more signs of radical discipleship than others in recent history, many have not connected their vertical relationship with God to their horizontal relationships with one another. Such connections don't necessarily come naturally, especially when it comes to loving those who are not like them. Like adults, kids need to be trained to make those connections.

While intervention by adults is the key to reaching traditional at-risk youth, peers are the keys to reaching ostracized and bullied kids. First, the numbers of such kids are so high that relying solely on adults would hardly begin to touch the tip of the iceberg. Second, most of us don't have the same access to such kids as the teenagers in our youth groups do. Our Christian teenagers are truly a significant part of the solution. Just as the viciousness of one youngster can send a child over the edge, the caring extended by another can begin to reverse all of that, bestowing a sense of worth and self-respect.

One seventeen-year-old girl understood this reality and expressed it eloquently in a recent "Letter to the Editor" of Newsweek magazine:

> *"Think about the average American high school. Think about the groups. The cliques. Now think about the students who are not in a group, not in a clique. The outsiders, the freaks, the weirdos, the geeks. To all my fellow students who may be reading this:* you *could prevent another tragedy from happening in your own seemingly safe school. Say hello to the guy who sits alone in chemistry and never speaks. Invite someone who always sits by herself at lunch to sit with you.*
>
> *"Think about what you are doing when you tease, laugh at or exclude someone from something just because he doesn't fit in. This may not solve the problem; some people are just not mentally stable. But if the youth in our schools make an effort to stop ostracizing such students, schools might become safer places. Maybe even happier, too."*[1]

HOW YOU KNOW WHEN YOU BELONG

All kids long for a place to belong. And they know whether or not they are welcome the moment they set foot in our youth groups:

First, they know they are welcome if one of their peers invites them. Apart from such an invitation, few will venture into strange territory and attempt to penetrate such an entirely foreign social system.

I remember well what life in the eighth grade was like. By then I had developed an ulcer because of excessive worry, anxiety, and a major inferiority complex. When it came to peers, I just didn't feel like I fit in. Struggling with depression and occasional thoughts of suicide, I was as at-risk as any youngster my age. I was very vulnerable at this point and could have gone in any number of directions, depending on who reached out to me first.

My parents were very concerned about me, and rightfully so. Therefore, they decided that I should attend a local Youth for Christ club. I resisted because I didn't know anybody there.

"You'll meet people once you get there," my mother assured me. "These are Christian kids. They'll make you feel welcome." I wasn't so convinced.

My mother dropped me off and went to the library, promising to pick me up promptly at 9:00. When I looked in the window and came to the terrifying conclusion that I didn't know a soul there, I actually made it to the library ahead of her. She demanded that I go back, but I refused. I would have opted for a torture chamber before walking into a strange group of kids where every eye would be focused on me. Try as she did to convince me otherwise, I went home with her, successfully avoiding the youth group meeting.

What happened in the weeks that followed baffles me to this day. I'm not sure if it was the result of my parents' fervent prayers or if they took a more active approach. Jim, a kid I sat next to in fourth period, invited me to a Youth for Christ meeting. What my mother could not accomplish through reasoning, coercion, or manipulation, Jim achieved in less than five minutes. From that point on, I never missed a meeting.

Second, kids know they are welcome when others in the youth group embrace them. When a young person who is ignored and excluded nearly every day at school suddenly feels welcome at a youth group, it is a powerful thing. The fact that so many of these kids have become engaged in negative groups is mostly because the negative groups were the first ones to reach out and embrace them.

When I first attended that youth group meeting, I knew no one. Though I recognized many of the faces from school, they were virtual strangers to me. Jim quickly introduced me to one or two of his friends, and I soon felt welcome. When I left that first night, I knew I had found a place where I belonged. It had nothing to do with spiritual convictions or a longing to grow in my faith; I simply felt welcome and accepted. The rest would come.

Third, kids feel they are welcome when they are given opportunities to lead and contribute to the group. Nobody likes to feel they are a mission field or project for someone else. Every act of kindness becomes suspect at that point.

Adults and youth subconsciously decide whether or not they are welcome in a group by how they answer the question, "Can I possibly contribute something to this group?" We may be able to get people to initially attend our programs, but if they cannot answer this question in the affirmative, it is unlikely they will continue for the long haul. Thus, slick and professional programs can actually be counterproductive if they cause kids to conclude that they are not really needed there.

Somehow the leader in that Youth for Christ program was mysteriously informed (thanks, Mom) that I played the guitar. He asked if I would be willing to play along the next week. They certainly didn't need another guitar in that group—I think they had five already—but once that director got me bringing my guitar, he had me committed. Now I *had* to attend. I was needed.

The best way to get fringe kids plugged into your program is to give them a responsibility: working in the sound room, setting up, greeting people, or taking the offering. Match them with jobs—important jobs— where they can succeed and that are consistent with their spiritual gifts. You'll find that they'll get far more out of your program than if they merely sat there passively. And they'll keep coming back.

INTEGRATING FRINGE KIDS

Simply getting fringe kids to attend a youth group event is not the same as integrating them into the life of the youth group. Below are some helpful ways to accomplish that very difficult task:

1. Establish a culture where kids genuinely love themselves and each other first. Young people cannot be expected to reach out to those outside the group if they have not yet learned to love themselves. The second greatest Commandment says as much, "Love your neighbor as yourself." It seems quite simple, but it is actually more difficult than at first glance. Because of insecurity, many kids detest or hate themselves, making it impossible for them to effectively reach out to their neighbors.

Just as a healthy self-image precedes being able to focus on the needs of others, loving those within our immediate circle is a prerequisite to reaching out to those beyond it.

TABATHA

Tabatha, who had always been more comfortable in the predictable world of adults, was unprepared for the severity of bullying she received when she reached eighth grade. She was frequently roughed up in the halls by other girls and called dirty names on a daily basis.

During that year she adopted the Gothic style of dress as an outward sign of her increasing estrangement from peers. Her melancholy rapidly shifted to rage. She began to fight back physically when teased or ridiculed and frequently found herself in the principal's office.

Early in her ninth grade year, she experienced a knockdown, dragout fight with four of her tormentors at the local shopping mall. At this point, her parents brought the problem to the attention of school officials. Tabatha reported to her therapist that she was constantly afraid at school, had no friends, and was thoroughly miserable. "Maybe the world would be better off without me," she reasoned.

Not knowing what else to do, Tabatha's parents urged her to join a local youth group. They persuaded her that this would give her a chance to meet youngsters under more positive circumstances.

"The church group was more depressing than school was because I expected more from it," Tabatha related. Students there also made fun of her appearance and style of dress. Under the very eye of the youth director, members leaned away from her and made faces, rolling their eyes whenever she ventured an opinion during Bible study.

"Knowing that even people who called themselves Christians rejected me made me feel worse than ever. But I suppose most of them weren't really there for God anyway. They were probably forced to attend, like me."

While Tabatha's assessment of that youth group might be true for many groups, such behavior is certainly not what today's kids are seeking to be part of, nor is it characteristic of youth groups that are growing.

2. Use larger events to introduce newer fringe kids to the group. It can be very intimidating for everyone involved when fringe kids are first introduced into a typical youth group meeting. It is threatening for the youth group kids because outsiders are treading on their safe and predictable turf. No one likes to have their own secure space invaded by newcomers. Likewise, it is intimidating for fringe kids coming in, as they can quickly discern that they are unwelcome and feel out of place.

Inviting new kids to special events at which nobody has a history allows all the kids to come together on common ground and bond through their shared experience. Such activities often involve extended periods of time as well, allowing for new relationships to be formed and deepened. The gelling that occurs is a byproduct of participating in a shared activity. Then when kids return to the youth group, it is more a matter of maintaining the momentum than trying to forge new relationships.

Some of the best events for facilitating this are "extreme activities" such as rafting, ropes courses, caving, snowboarding, or service projects. The purpose of these activities is to take kids into an alien environment and push them a little beyond their comfort zones. We need to purposely plan such events, for they don't naturally happen in the course of normal church life.

One of the great things about mission trips is that they level the playing field for everyone involved. I recall looking at photos of teams of young people we have taken on such trips. In the departure photos, our hair was neatly arranged and our clothes spotless. We looked good, but our eyes always revealed a level of insecurity and self-absorption. What a difference when compared to photos shot toward the end of a trip. After days without showers, clean clothes, or hair dryers, our outward appearances weren't nearly so attractive, but our eyes looked altogether different. They sparkled. For many, it was the first time they had ever felt so wanted or needed or important.

Events like these also provide kids with benchmarks and milestones which they can look back on. In 1 Samuel 7:12, the prophet Samuel "took a stone and set it up between Mizpah and Shen. He called it Ebenezer, saying, 'Thus far has the Lord helped us.' " Such "Ebenezers" are so critical for kids because from that time on, they can recall with laughter and meaning events from past camps, retreats, or wild activities.

DAVE

Quiet, shy, and overweight, Dave was accustomed to being the butt of countless jokes. Away from the crowds, though, he had a keen sense of humor and possessed incredible amounts of talent and creativity. It was a side of him that few saw because he had learned that the best way to survive was to hide from the spotlight and avoid any attention. For Dave, attention was always closely linked to humiliation.

One of our staff members, John, led a group of kids on a mission trip to Jamaica a few years ago. Dave was on that trip.

"A whole new Dave emerged in Jamaica," recalls John. "Some of the groups that had arrived from different parts of the United States were having difficulty gelling. Dave arose as sort of the 'MC' of the whole group. Everyone saw him as the fun, caring kid with the Boston accent—not as the fat, quiet kid everyone made fun of. The transformation was incredible.

"When Dave wasn't around, others would look for him. A hard worker and a soother of the hurting, he was also shedding the chains that had so tightly bound him. He even got up to participate in the talent show the last night.

"When we got back, everyone was amazed when Dave got up in front of the youth group to share his experiences. For the first time, they were laughing with him and not at him. He still got teased after that, but he was able to put up with it and to stick up for himself when he needed to. He never retreated back into the cocoon that had always smothered him before."

What brought about such change? Acceptance by a group of peers, responsibility placed upon him by his leaders, and a place where he felt safe enough to reveal himself to others. And when others saw who he really was, instead of who he wasn't, they liked him. As is often the case, it took getting them out of their normal environment to reveal what was there all along.

3. Establish clear rules and boundaries at youth group events. Much of the frustration of integrating fringe kids into youth groups involves the assumed expectations held by each person. The regulars want it to be like it was, but new kids have no idea what that means. This requires making the expectations clear. When new kids break the rules, don't embarrass them publicly; speak with them in private.

Even more effective is when other youth in the group simply exhibit proper conduct despite the more aberrant behavior some may be displaying. Kids quickly notice what is acceptable and what is not and tend to adjust accordingly to fit in.

One of the best bullying prevention techniques is to talk frankly and honestly with the kids. First, ask them to define what acts constitute bullying. As they come up with things like gossiping, mocking, public humiliation, name-calling, dirty looks, and exclusion, ask how many had received such treatment in the past year. Then ask how big a problem they think bullying is in your youth group.

Once people agree on the problem, invite suggestions as to how they might covenant to prevent such harmful acts in the future. As youth take ownership in both the problem and the solution, they will also be much more committed to the process of stopping such activities. This also provides a platform to come back to if the problem resurfaces.

BRIAN

Mike, a local youth leader, told me how one of his kids, Brian, was continually picking on younger, smaller kids in the program. Mike had confronted Brian on numerous occasions, but to absolutely no avail. He even spoke to Brian's parents and threatened to kick him out of the group.

When sign-up time came for the fall youth retreat, Brian's name was at the top of the list. "We can't let him go or I'll be chasing him all weekend," was Mike's first thought. But after praying about it, he didn't feel it would be right to ban Brian from the retreat. Instead, on the opening night, he clearly laid out the ground rules for the weekend, including mistreatment of kids.

As Mike explained that everyone was responsible for the climate of the group, kids seemed to understand. He asked for their input on what behaviors constituted bullying and invited ideas on how it should be addressed. There was no mention of names, but later that evening when Brian started picking on someone, his friends stepped in to confront him.

"You're turning my friends against me!" accused Brian, as he angrily confronted Mike later that evening. Mike again explained why his actions were unacceptable and why nobody in the youth group would tolerate them. "If somebody picks on you, we would be there in your defense as well," he assured Brian.

The next evening, a frustrated Brian finally broke down in tears. He confessed how he had been brutalized by an older brother all his life, and that he had assumed that acting in such a manner was the only way he could feel good about himself.

From time to time, Brian would sink back into old patterns, but each time his peers would either say something or simply give him a disapproving look. That was all it took for him to stop. The youth group was able to do something no one else could do. They helped Brian break a pattern he had been entrenched in since childhood. Much to his surprise, the group hadn't rejected him for his actions, but instead embraced him through loving confrontation.

4. Create an environment where kids can encounter Christ. Kids today need more than just to know *about* God. They need to *encounter* and *experience* him in a way that connects personally with them. When I was in high school, we spent lots of time studying apologetics. We knew that if our friends were going to seriously consider the claims of Christ, we had to present a logical argument for our faith. For teenagers living in these postmodern times, however, understanding isn't believing. Seeing or feeling is believing. It is common to hear today's youth say things like, "It *felt* good here tonight. I'll be back."

Outcast and fringe kids tend to be more aware of their own deep needs than most. One reason is that many are wounded and asking questions that others don't begin to consider until much later in life, such as "Is there really a God?" "What is the meaning of life?" and "Why am I here?" A searching attitude has always been a prerequisite to powerful encounters with Jesus. His style was not to give long sermons, but rather to offer invitations to the needy as in John 7:37: "If anyone is thirsty, let him [or her] come to me and drink." Outcast kids are primed for such an invitation from Jesus. Our youth groups should offer no less.

The Responsiveness of Samaritans

Though the Samaritans were one of the most ridiculed, ostracized, and neglected groups in New Testament times, they actually responded more favorably than most of the people Jesus encountered. Of the ten lepers he healed in Luke 17, only one came back to thank him. He was a Samaritan.

Some of his most fruitful ministry came through a Samaritan woman he met at a well. John reports that within just a couple of days "a great number of people believed because of her faith."

It wasn't until mass persecution broke out in Jerusalem against the apostles that they finally ventured into Samaria. Acts 8 chronicles some of the amazing accounts of what happened there. Mighty miracles were performed, evil spirits were cast out, large numbers were healed, and great joy filled the city. Though Philip was the only apostle commissioned there, Peter and John soon followed because of the overwhelming response.

Fringe kids have a great deal in common with the Samaritans of Jesus' day. Not only are they easily passed over by those in the mainstream, but they are often the most responsive to the message of Christ.

5. Start early. Bullying behavior begins as soon as children begin to sense the differences between themselves and their peers. Hence some of the cruelest attacks occur in elementary schools, as evidenced by the following note handed to a classmate by eight-year-old Wanda.

Awful Janet

Your the stinkiest girl in this world. I hope you die but of course I suppose that's impossible. I've got some ideas.
1. Play in the road
2. Cut your throad
3. Drink poison
4. get drunk
5. knife yourself
Please do some of this you big fat Girl. we all hate you. I'm praying Oh please lord let Janet die. Were in need of fresh air. Did you hear me lord cause if you didn't will all die with her here. See Janet we're not all bad.

From Wanda Jackson[2]

One of the best ways to get an anti-bullying message to the younger children of a church is through the older teenagers. Because children look to older peers to learn acceptable patterns of behavior, teenagers are in a unique position to give instruction, especially when it comes to how one treats peers.

Having the youth group plan a presentation for the Sunday school classes (first through eighth grades) using skits, puppets, or stories is a most effective means of teaching kids early that bullying is destructive and wrong. At the same time, the esteem of youth group members is increased and the concepts become more ingrained as they take on the role of "teachers."

deploying christian youth

"These are the best years of your life. Enjoy them while you can. Things only go downhill from here." I remember how much I hated people telling me that as a teenager. I wasn't very enthusiastic about my teenage years, so such a statement didn't exactly excite me about the future.

While some thrive in middle and high school, for most it is a combination of some wonderful times interspersed with lots of anxiety, confusion, and stress. Adolescent insecurities, susceptibility to peer influence, and identity struggles have made the teenage years difficult ones for all who have passed through them.

Perhaps the main reason these years are difficult is the fact that everything is so amplified during adolescence. The highs are higher and the lows lower. To the teenager, everything is gigantic. A teacher's kind word, a dirty look from a former best friend across the cafeteria, a pimple, or the realization that one could walk down the hallway and not have anyone say "hi" all seem like matters of life and death for a teenager. They feel like every eye is on them.

John Hoover's teenage daughter would complain when the family joked around in restaurants, shushing them and saying, "Everyone's looking at us!" A quick glance around the restaurant, however, would reveal that nobody else was even remotely tuned in to their conversation.

Not only are teenagers unusually self-absorbed, but modern technology is also validating what most of us have suspected for a long time: that it is extremely difficult for teenagers to think logically. Neuroscientists have actually confirmed that the last part of the brain to develop is the region that enables us to handle ambiguous information and make logical, coherent decisions.

The prefrontal cortex, that part of the brain where sound judgments are formed, is not fully developed in most people until their early twenties.

Meanwhile, the limbic system, where raw emotions such as anger are generated, is entering a stage of hyperdevelopment, explaining at least in part how teenagers can be so moody, apparently making decisions based solely on emotions.[1]

Add to that, the fact that in boys, testosterone levels in the bloodstream rise a hundredfold during puberty.[2] Is it any wonder that they struggle to make coherent decisions while under the influence of such a potent chemical that fuels both sex and aggression?

While teenagers may be limited in some of their cognitive abilities, they are exceedingly aware of the culture around them. In every venue they enter, they know instinctively whether or not they belong. Not surprisingly, they spend most of their time in places and with people where they feel most comfortable. Thus, the "culture" of our youth group is just as important as the lessons we teach. But how do we help self-absorbed youth group kids begin to look beyond their own interests and insecurities?

Jesus prescribed a cure for this condition when he said, "Whoever wants to save his life will lose it, but whoever loses his life for me will save it" (Luke 9:24). Paradoxically, it is in this process of looking beyond ourselves to the needs of others that we find a sense of identity and security.

Henri Nouwen discovered this when he left Harvard University to minister among the mentally disabled at L'Arche Daybreak Community in Toronto. There he wrote, "For anyone who has the courage to enter our human sorrows deeply, there is a revelation of joy, hidden like a precious stone in the wall of a dark cave."[3]

Though critically important, this process does not just happen naturally for young people. It begins with our teaching and is illustrated through our actions, but it is not grasped until kids are given the opportunity to experience it for themselves.

Reaching out to those who may be unappealing is difficult for mature Christians, let alone youngsters just starting down the path. But to be biblical Christians demands that we:

1. Spread the gospel to Gentiles. This specifically includes those who are not part of the "in" group. For first century Jews, Gentiles possessed the ultimate outsider status. Even the Apostle Peter was repulsed at the thought of succumbing to Gentile eating practices as he gasped, "Surely not, Lord!" (Acts 10:14). And this was after God had clearly directed him to do so in a vision.

Christ's nature, fully God and fully man, meant that he shared many things with us. But it also meant that every person he touched was fundamentally different from him. Ironically, Jesus gathered to himself prostitutes and tax collectors, while being quarrelsome with the most respectable members of his own community. As he himself phrased it with his actions, "I came to save sinners, not the righteous." Or as one pundit rephrased it, "Jesus came to comfort the afflicted and to afflict the comfortable."

2. Comfort the weak, hurting, and vulnerable. Throughout Scripture God actively seeks out at least five distinct types of people: the poor, the sick, the orphan, the widow, and the imprisoned. Here is where God's heart beats loudest. If you desire to have your heart in sync with his, start hanging out with fringe kids. Most of them fit into several of these categories.

Romans 12:16 also demands that we not be proud or conceited but be willing to associate with people of "low" position. In middle and secondary schools, the low ones certainly are easily identified. They are the ones who regularly face rejection and bullying. A criticism of the early church was that it was a religion for slaves—those considered undesirable. It still is, or should be.

3. Act out faith through a life of service to others. A central calling for Christians is to demonstrate Christ's earthly body through service to others. Every other thing we enjoy on this earth as Christians will be infinitely better in heaven: the worship better, the fellowship richer, the teaching out of this world. The only thing we can do here that we cannot do in heaven is serve those who don't yet know Christ and be a testimony of his love for them by our words and actions.

Overseas mission trips and local work with the homeless, shut-ins, or other needy people is essential. But who thinks of ministering to picked-on kids in school as an outreach of love? It ought to be a core component of every youth group program.

4. Understand and accept cultural differences. Early Christians disputed about whether converts needed to become Jews before they could be Christianized. After many debates, the first truly "cross-cultural" ministry was birthed when the Jerusalem Council determined that gentiles who came to faith in Christ did not need to become cultural Jews to be members of the early church.

In the same way, youth and adults must be challenged to accept different and even troubling behavior on the part of those with whom they work. Our goal is not to make kids culturally like us or even to change their behavior. The latter can only begin to happen because of inner changes wrought by the Holy Spirit.

KIDS CATCHING THE VISION

We had just returned from a powerful retreat with the first youth group I worked with. I was exhausted, but it was a good kind of tired. Several kids had made significant commitments to Christ.

That's why I wasn't too shocked when Randy, Tom, and Joe stopped by my house the following week to inform me of their plans. "We want to get together for prayer every morning before school."

"That's wonderful!" I exclaimed.

"We thought since you live right across from the high school we might do it at your house," they continued in their exuberance.

"Well, uh, what time were you thinking about meeting?"

"At 6:30 since we have to be at school by 7:10," they explained.

My job as a stockbroker and the work I was doing with Youth for Christ kept me up late into the evenings, so I rarely arose before 7:00. I might have objected to their proposal except that I didn't want to discourage them. And in the back of my mind, I thought that such a commitment would probably be short-lived anyway.

I was so skeptical, I didn't even bother changing my alarm clock setting. At 6:25 the next morning, I was awakened by my doorbell. The three of them looked somewhat shocked and mildly disappointed that I hadn't placed more faith in their pledge.

We met that morning to read a few verses from 1 John and to pray. No one was more surprised than I was when that small band continued to come day after day. It was a genuine act of God, as the group grew from three to twelve.

Even more indicative of divine rumblings was how their prayer requests changed over the course of those months. At first they were the typical, "Pray for my third period math test. I didn't get much time to study." But in time they began to shift to, "Pray for Tony, a kid in my humanities class who everyone picks on. It makes me sick to watch, but I don't know what to do about it." And, "I'm sad about Tony, too, Lord. Please show us what we can do about that situation. It's just not right, and I know it breaks your heart even more than it does ours."

Such hearts and prayers carried the imprints of revival all over them. As we struggled through such issues, our little Youth for Christ club was transformed. Kids were becoming committed to ministering to the lost and "the least" in their midst. The youth group soon grew substantially in size, but more than that, those who had largely felt displaced suddenly had a place where they belonged and felt embraced. Virtually all of them eventually made commitments to Christ and some even went on to full-time Christian service.

To truly reflect the heart of God, every youth group must struggle through issues of what they can and dare do. Following are some of the steps we, as youth group leaders, can take to start such a process.

1. Pray for broken hearts. Before kids will ever risk reaching beyond their own selfish needs and insecurities, having their hearts broken is an absolute prerequisite. By this we mean having hearts full of compassion and empathy. In fact, attempting to "guilt" kids into reaching out is a waste of time if God hasn't begun doing a significant work in their hearts. It wasn't until a few of our kids started praying and drawing near to God that their hearts became convicted over the need for them to reach out to *the lost* and *the least*.

That's why the Great Commandment, to love the Lord with all your heart, soul, and mind (Matthew 22:37), precedes the Great Commission, to go and make disciples (Matthew 28:19). Then, as we do go, Acts 1:8 lays out a strategy to reach the whole world, but it begins at home in Jerusalem. The "Jerusalem" for kids is their humanities class and cafeteria.

2. Model reaching out. Kids observe what we do much more than they listen to what we say. When they see us embracing and making a big deal over newcomers, they are much more inclined to do the same. Likewise, when we schedule all of our time with the same group of kids, it illustrates an attitude toward newcomers that our kids are quick to pick up on.

Not only must we model reaching out, but we are also responsible for the climate in the group. When adults turn a blind eye toward bullying, two equally unfortunate things happen. First, a hidden curriculum is taught to bullies and bystanders; namely, that using one person for another's amusement is acceptable behavior. Second, the victim status conferred upon an individual becomes solidified, making the further bullying of that person all but guaranteed. For adults to stand by and watch, or to turn away and ignore, is to participate in the abuse of children as surely as if they had hurled the insults themselves.

3. Equip kids to reach out. After our little band of prayer warriors had their hearts broken for their hurting peers, they were perplexed about what they could do. All kids need training in how to effectively reach out to those around them. Appendix 1 contains a six-week youth group series that can be effectively used to help accomplish that very task.

Deploying Christian youth to disciple fringe kids involves several steps. These are discussed throughout the book, but their order is significant:

1. Challenge Christian youth with the biblical commandment to love others, using passages like the parable of the good Samaritan in Luke 10 or the sheep and the goats in Matthew 25.

2. Emphasize the need to perform ministry close to home before launching out across the globe. Acts 1:8 can be particularly helpful in explaining the difference between "Jerusalem," "Judea," "Samaria" and the "ends of the earth," and why their order is significant.

3. Prepare young people to carry out the task. That training should include:

• Fervent prayer so that young people can learn to hear God's voice as he leads them into opportunities to reach out, as well as to confront bullying behavior.

• Understanding the "frames and phrases" approach for confronting bullying. (See Chapter 6.)

• Demonstrating and modeling ways to approach devalued youth. Having youth role-play these, analyze them, and report back on their progress can be helpful.

4. Working to create a youth group climate that is both respectful and inviting to outsiders.

5. Recognizing and rewarding ministering to others so long as it does not become competitive or disrespectful to those you are trying to reach.

4. Commission them. We make a big deal about kids going on short-term mission trips, and rightly so. It has always been more enticing to go to the "ends of the earth" (for a week or two), than to labor back in "Jerusalem" or "Samaria" day after day. Yet worldwide impact that does not either originate out of one's local influence, or spill over into it, is suspect at best.

Part of the reason most kids don't think about their campus in such a way is that we don't challenge them to do so. Why not have commissioning ceremonies for ministering love and peace on campuses like we do for other mission trips? I was with one youth pastor recently whose youth group consists of fifty kids who represent twenty-four different high school campuses. He is training his students to see these campuses as mission fields for their youth group. Each week they focus on a different one, both in prayer and in hearing from students about what God is doing there and what the obstacles are.

For some kids, the challenge of witnessing to six of their nonbelieving friends over the next year would be out of the question, but asking them to befriend the friendless or to love the unloved and unlovable are tasks that can be done by anyone. Such a challenge does not demand an extroverted or bold personality. Being willing to simply watch with prayerful hearts and to reach out in love allows every young person to have a significant ministry and to be personally changed in the process.

5. Confront injustice on school campuses. In the aftermath of Littleton, Colorado, Washington Post reporters Lorraine Adams and Dale Russakoff began investigating the claims of "jockism" running rampant at Columbine High School, and the role it may have played in the massacre. They reported:

The state wrestling champ was regularly permitted to park his $100,000 Hummer all day in a fifteen-minute space. A football player was allowed to tease a girl about her breasts in class without fear of retribution by his teacher, who was also his coach. Dozens of interviews and a review of court records show that Harris and Klebold knew of instances where athletes convicted of crimes went without suspension from games or expulsion from school. They witnessed instances of athletes tormenting others while school officials looked the other way. They believed that high-profile athletes could finagle their way out of jail.[4]

Throughout history, the church's brightest moments have occurred when it was willing to confront society's injustices. The church's role in abolishing slavery in England, as well as the establishment of hospitals and homeless missions in poverty-stricken areas, is all part of its rich heritage. From the very first century, even fiery opponents of the church like Lucian of Samosata had to concede, "During outbreaks of the plague, these Christians tend the sick and bury the dead even when everyone else has fled!"[5]

Are today's young people up for the challenge of confronting injustices such as jockism on their own campuses? I believe so.

THE ROLE OF PEER PRESSURE

Whenever we talk with teenagers about the need to reach out to bullied kids, the topic of peer pressure inevitably comes up. "I'm worried about what other people will think about me if I start talking to those people," one girl explained to me.

Certainly peer pressure looms large in the mind of every young person. Nobody wants to stand out or to be different. But as I look back on my own years of growing up, it was the people who had the guts to stand out and be different who most influenced me for good.

CHIP

Chip had a character trait that makes him stand out in my mind even decades later. I cannot recall him ever complaining or speaking negatively about anyone. He always seemed to be positive, a unique characteristic for anyone, but especially for a teenager. To this day, whenever I hear the words from Ephesians 4:29, "Do not let any unwholesome talk come out of your mouths, but only what is helpful for building others up," I immediately think of Chip.

One summer I was privileged to be a fellow camper in his cabin at a summer camp. Typical of boys' cabins, our conversation was filled with crude sarcasm, brutal put-downs, and degrading comments about the girls at the camp. Chip never confronted us, but he was noticeably silent when it came to participating.

The thing that stands out in my mind years later is how his silence changed the climate of our cabin. By the end of the week the gossip had literally ceased, which I contribute solely to the influence of Chip. Teenagers are looking for people to follow, so why not challenge them to follow people like Chip? Contrary to what they might expect, they will likely be more respected by their peers rather than less.

Whenever kids are willing to stand against the tide of peer pressure it has an impact. Sometimes the impact is more profound than others.

DARYL

One Friday night, my high school friends and I were driving through a rival school town. At a stoplight, a carload of kids pulled alongside us. One of them extended his middle finger toward us, accompanied by a degrading string of profanity. Our tempers were immediately ignited and we responded in an even ranker fashion determined to put them in their place. Just then, the light turned green.

For the next several miles, fists and upper bodies hung out of windows as we raced nose to nose down the highway. Only one thing curtailed the impending fight straining to ensue. It was Daryl, the driver of our car.

"Pull over!" we screamed at him as he drove onto the interstate highway heading home. I wasn't particularly prone to fights, but with our state's heavyweight wrestling champion in the back seat, I was talking as tough as anyone. Finally, the other kids tired of the chase and, with appropriate gestures, exited the highway.

Daryl took a good bit of abuse from the three of us as we headed back home. "Why were you being such a wuss?! We could have taken them easy!"

It wasn't until years later that I apologized and thanked him for having the guts to not give in to us. I have met scores of kids who were in similar predicaments and who are now serving time in prison for similar acts done with friends where there was no Daryl present to stop them. I am convinced that with teenage tempers as hot as they were that night, a crowbar in a trunk or a baseball bat in a back seat may well have put somebody in the hospital or worse. Standing up does take guts. Thank God for gutsy teenagers!

HEROIC ACTS OF COURAGE

Every youth group has kids like Daryl and Chip. Our job is to turn the spotlight on them and to elevate such acts of courage. One way is to officially recognize such heroic decisions. At meetings, have occasional times for sharing the courageous acts different youth members have done—from the small ones to the large ones. Adults can regularly share stories from their own lives as well, like those of Daryl and Chip.

Some youth groups even have a wall where teenagers nominate one another for acts of kindness or courage. The benefits for those who commit such valiant acts go far beyond mere prizes.

STRINGBEAN

By eighth grade I had finally earned the right to sit in the back seat of the school bus. I thought I had "arrived" and milked it for all it was worth.

Halfway through the school year, a new boy got on our bus. I don't actually remember his name, only that we called him Stringbean because he was so tall and skinny.

An acne-faced, quiet, unattractive kid, Stringbean made a grave mistake the first day he arrived. He sat in the front seat of the bus, immediately confirming in our minds that he was a nerd who needed to be taught a lesson. We began shooting spitwads at him, tipping books out of his hands as he walked, and yelling "Stringbean!" whenever we came upon him in the hallways.

Being a Christian, I felt a twinge of guilt at how I was treating him. I recall telling my mother about it. "You should feel guilty, Scott. That's just plain wrong!" she said. "Maybe you should invite him over for dinner."

Well, I wasn't sure I felt that guilty.

I did begin feeling more and more convicted about it, though. I stopped joining in on the attacks against Stringbean, but the pattern of abuse had already been set.

One day I decided to make what would be one of the boldest moves of my adolescent years. I sat next to Stringbean in the cafeteria. I thought he would be elated to have a companion, but he didn't say. After a few times of sitting together, I found that he had already lived in thirteen different foster homes. I apologized for how I had treated him when he first came to our school. "Oh, that's all right," he said, "That's pretty much how everyone treats me." That made me feel worse.

I started hanging out with Stringbean more and more. He never sat in the back of the bus, but I would occasionally sit in the front seat with him—not to be a nice guy, but because I enjoyed his company. An amazing thing began to happen: My friends eventually stopped picking on him too. I had never told them to stop, they just picked up on what I was doing.

Something began to change in me, as well. It was the first time I had ever stood up for anything as a teenager. I didn't think I could even do it, much less that it would make a difference. I was wrong on both fronts. My heart was also becoming broken for kids that others seemed to pass by. As an eighth grader I became conscious of the other "Stringbeans" in my school too.

Then one morning when our bus stopped at his house, Stringbean didn't get on. He didn't get on the next day either, or the one after that. When I asked his foster sister what had happened to him, she said he had been transferred to a different foster home.

I never saw Stringbean again, but the influence he had on my life would be long-standing. Some of my own teenage insecurity was overcome by shifting my focus off me and onto him. I also learned that I could make a difference in my school and in the life of someone else. I also credit him as part of the reason I chose to enter a ministry with troubled and hurting kids.

commissioning outcast kids to a high calling

When Tim came to Trinity Church as youth pastor he had a heart for all kids, but especially the fringe ones. He had learned from his previous ministry the importance of instilling such a vision into his adult and youth leadership before launching out on his own.

The youth group at Trinity was unusually mature and ready to follow Tim's lead in reaching out. They began to work hard to create an environment where hurting kids felt safe and accepted.

Marty was the first fringe kid Trinity really reached out to. One of the youth group regulars had invited him. Marty grew up on the wrong side of the tracks, at least in comparison to the rest of the kids in the youth group. He wasn't a troublemaker, although it was well known that he came from a troubled family. Even though there was no father in the house, there was no shortage of men coming and going. His mother worked as a waitress and carried the curse of a bad reputation in town, which began back when she was in high school. Each of her three children had different fathers, none of whom claimed their children.

The oldest brother had been a fighter and carouser. In and out of detention centers, he finally joined the army after graduation. No one was too sad to see him go.

Marty was altogether different, though. He more or less lived in his own shell. Much slighter in body than his older brother, he wasn't the type to fight back, making him a prime target for bullies. Though he might have been ridiculed for his family background or neighborhood, names like "homo" and "faggot" were the ones that stuck, accentuating his more effeminate mannerisms.

That's why it was so significant that the youth group reached out and included Marty. And he thrived there. One night after youth group the kids were all outside doing "all-star wrestling" moves. Marty was fitting right in with all the roughhousing and joking around. Tom, one of the more popular kids, took Marty's head and pushed it down as he brought his knee up. Tom meant to stop, but his knee whacked Marty in the nose. Everyone was laughing, except Marty. Tears welled up in Marty's eyes as he walked away.

One of the leaders saw what had happened and followed him. By now Marty was crying hard. Tom came over and apologized, too, but the damage to a sensitive ego was already done. When Tim, the youth pastor, brought Marty home, he tried to get him to talk about what had happened, but he was inconsolable and wouldn't talk. Marty never came back to youth group again.

Everyone felt bad about it. Some blamed Tom for letting things get so out of control. Others felt guilty for laughing at Marty, not having realized that he was really hurt. Most were frustrated that after all they had done for Marty he would so easily write them off. They felt that if Marty wanted to be that way, fine.

For kids like Marty, a seemingly small embarrassment can be monumental. Had someone like Tom been the one kneed in the head, he might have shed a few tears and been a little embarrassed, but he would have returned the next week unscathed. But for someone who saw himself as the "wimpy little queer boy," the humiliation of shedding tears in front of cool kids was more than he could bear. Trinity Church was discovering that there was a lot more involved in ministering to bullied kids than merely getting them to attend youth group.

For outcast young people to develop into healthy adults, several things must happen. First, they need opportunities to process their feelings about the past. Second, they must learn to be assertive and stand up for themselves. Third, they must learn to forgive. Fourth, they must be equipped and commissioned to reach others. And finally, they need significant responsibilities within the youth group and the church.

PROCESSING THE PAST

Teenagers who have experienced the ravages of peer rejection and persecution have often been injured in profound ways. Don't expect them to respond quickly or easily, as these issues can be very shameful or embarrassing for them to express. At the same time, however, they long for someone with whom to process their feelings. The following steps can be helpful for facilitating such a dialogue:

1. LISTEN — When a young person begins to open up, it is imperative that at first we just listen, avoiding the temptation to give advice or to minimize their pain. Making eye contact, leaning toward them, not acting shocked at what they say, and occasionally asking pertinent questions are all evidence of good listening skills.

2. EMPATHIZE — Most young people in pain are convinced that no one really understands how they feel. Briefly relaying similar situations from our own experience can help so long as we don't dwell on our stories. Teenagers tend to be very self-focused and quickly lose interest when the story suddenly shifts from them to us. Statements that paraphrase what we sense they may be going through can help make the connection.

3. AFFIRM — It is very important to affirm a young person's value and worth, especially after they have shared things for which they may be embarrassed or ashamed. Hope is imparted not by telling kids to have hope, but through our unswerving commitment to them. Once they are convinced of our love and belief in them, they can begin to develop their own sense of hope.

4. ENLIST — Involving teenagers in their own problem-solving process is a good way to empower and equip them. It is important that we help them think through all the options before them, as kids say that they feel they have a say in what happens to them only 20 percent of the time. Then when *they* choose a plan of action, we are also in a position to help them stick to it.[1]

LEARNING ASSERTIVENESS

Once kids are convinced that we understand what they are going through, they are more likely to trust us with teaching them skills for dealing with their problems. One of the most needed skills of badgered kids is assertiveness training.

Most kids who have been bullied appear very timid and afraid. Unfortunately, in the world of schoolyard bullies, children who act like victims generally remain victims. How do we help them "turn the other cheek" without turning them into doormats and inviting more abuse? Jesus' admonition was not a call to weakness but to strength and confidence. Thus, such kids need help in becoming more assertive and believing they are worthy enough to shed the victim status. Admittedly, this is easier said than done. For many, it involves unlearning a lifetime of patterns.

Assertiveness training is best done in a one-on-one discipling relationship with a trusted adult. Here are some basic skills that can be taught to a bullied youth. Instruct them to:

1. Use a firm voice without a quivering or tremulous tone. The volume should be loud, but not shouting.

2. State what you want in specific terms such as, "I want you to leave me alone when I walk by here from now on." The time and place to deliver such a message is of utmost importance. You should not be alone nor should you be in the presence of people who could cause the bully's pride to be threatened.

3. Have a well thought out plan in case the bully resists or challenges your request. Having adults or peers nearby who will speak up on your behalf, standing by you and your demands, is critical.

4. Be persistent. Most bullies eventually get the point that their behavior will not be tolerated and stop their bullying.

FORGIVING

Once kids have grasped the assertiveness stage, it is important for them to begin moving toward authentic forgiveness. Apart from that, they can never be completely free. The issue is not whether the offender deserves forgiveness. Rather, it is because of Christ's forgiveness toward us that we are able to extend forgiveness to others.

Though not easy, this is a foundational teaching of Jesus. The Lord's prayer states, "Forgive us our trespasses, as we forgive those who trespass against us." Said another place even more explicitly, "If you do not forgive men their sins, your father will not forgive your sins" (Matthew 6:15).

This is not to suggest that the act of forgiveness is painless. Kids should not be made to feel excessive guilt when they still harbor occasional feelings of hurt, anger, or even hate, especially for wounds that are deep. Because forgiveness is a process, it is often two steps forward and one step back.

By encouraging forgiveness, we are not asking kids to ignore their abuser's actions or to allow them to continue. That is enabling. Forgiveness is a process—a supernatural one at that—whereby we entrust ourselves, as well as our perpetrators, into the hands of God, releasing them from retaliation and wishing them well.

TANYA

Tanya was a girl who had suffered a great deal of verbal and emotional abuse from her father. She became very angry at my suggestion that we all must be willing to forgive. After youth group she blasted me, saying, "You have no idea what I've been through. I've vowed never to speak to my father again, let alone forgive him!"

I didn't preach at her but just listened, and prayed. But God was working in Tanya's heart. She was the one who brought it up again months later: "The hatred I feel for my father is killing me, but I don't feel like I could ever forgive him."

I assured her that her statement meant she was already well along in the process. I explained that a good next step might be to simply ask God to give her the desire to *want* to forgive him. That began a miraculous process that culminated several months later.

Tanya explained, "I know my father felt awkward being around me, too, because whenever we were in the same room, the air was so thick you could cut it. One night it was just the two of us in the living room watching TV after everyone had gone to bed. I suddenly felt incredibly sorry for him, for the first time in my life. I went to get him a glass of soda and when I handed it to him, I looked at him and started to cry. I couldn't stop for a long time. We hugged each other and I told him I loved him. He said he loved me, too, and asked me to forgive him. I said, 'I forgive you, Daddy.' It was the greatest day of my life."

No matter how many positive skills we introduce into a young person's life, until he or she effectively deals with issues of the past—specifically the forgiveness of self and others—true freedom can never be fully realized. As hard as it is to forgive someone else, forgiving ourselves can be even more difficult.

JIMMY

Already locked up for nineteen years, Jimmy has no hope of ever getting out. Abused and picked on as a kid, he committed his crime of revenge at eighteen years of age. When he felt he could take no more, he fought back and ultimately killed one of his abusers. Now he has the rest of his life to deal with the fallout of that decision.

After more than a decade of incarceration Jimmy finally decided to move beyond a helpless "woe is me" attitude and begin seriously dealing with some of the issues that had landed him in prison. As a result, he became heavily involved in church and Narcotics Anonymous (NA).

"When I got to Step Four in the Twelve Steps to Recovery, it required my taking a brutally honest inventory of my life," recalls Jimmy. "The particular NA curriculum I was using involved answering 166 questions. Those questions were designed to shine the light into every corner of your life.

"My sponsor suggested I write for about an hour and a half each day, and then put it away until the next day. When I read what I had written the first day, I said to myself, 'This isn't exactly how it really was.' So I tore it up and started writing again. The following day when I reviewed my work, I could see I still wasn't being completely honest. So once again I ripped it up and started over.

"I couldn't believe the power of self-deceit. I wasn't even able to tell myself the truth! This process continued for three and a half months. Finally, I had produced twenty-three pages of brutally honest responses to those 166 questions.

"Step Five requires you to read your answers to another person. I held off on this one for awhile, but, in time, I found another inmate who had been working through the same program. After reading him my twenty-three pages, he asked me to hear his. When we were finished, we burned the pages as was suggested in the curriculum.

"The amazing thing is that since then, I have said every one of those things publicly, either in my small group Bible study or at an NA meeting. They no longer have a hold on me. I feel like I'm finally free!"

Contrast that with a prisoner I encountered a month before at a women's prison where I was teaching a seminar. While I was in the waiting area, the alarm went off. Within minutes, a fleet of police cars and an ambulance pulled up as several officers charged in.

Soon we heard blood-curdling shrieks, as a young woman, tied down on a metal stretcher with wheels, appeared. Her neck and arms were bandaged and she was screaming at the top of her lungs, "Let me die! Let me die!" Later that evening she was brought back from the hospital to the prison and placed under twenty-four-hour suicide watch, her four limbs tied to the corners of the cell.

I later learned that she had been imprisoned for kidnapping her children from a foster home where they had been placed. In the ensuing chase with police, she had a car accident, and both children were killed. Now she has twenty-four hours a day in a prison cell to ponder such horrors. I can understand why she wanted to die. I would too. Forgiveness is what she so desperately needed. And forgiveness is what we have to offer people through Jesus Christ.

COMMISSIONED TO A HIGHER CALLING

We must be careful about focusing only on the problems fringe kids face. As long as we are consumed with just helping them, they remain a mere project, and nobody likes to be someone else's project. All youth need a challenge big enough to be worthy of their lives, but especially those who have felt ostracized or abandoned. As one young man's suicide note read, "Not having a good enough reason to live is a good enough reason to die."

It is critical for kids to focus outside themselves and gain a clearer sense of purpose for their lives. As they begin to gain a greater sense of God's calling on their lives, many of the other issues plaguing them begin to fade by comparison.

Most kids who are bullied attain a sense of purpose once they finish high school and discover that physical appearance and athletic ability are not the only keys to success. In the meantime, having opportunities to recognize and use their talents and abilities makes the journey a whole lot easier.

I have observed that many of my classmates who skated through adolescence with relative ease, enjoying the benefits of natural talent and popularity, have not fared so well since. Though they appeared promising in high school, many flunked out in life. Because of not needing to work hard at athletics or academics, many did not develop the skills or tenacity necessary to progress beyond their present circumstances. On the other hand, those who were forced to work hard were more likely to develop determination and perseverance.

Like the chick pecking through its shell, or the butterfly coming out of its cocoon, that difficult work prepares and strengthens. Without it, the chick or butterfly would be too weak to thrive or even survive.

ASSUMING RESPONSIBILITY

We noted earlier that people tend to judge whether they fit into a church or youth group by whether or not they envision being able to assume responsibilities there. When those who hold responsibilities in the group have a very homogeneous look to them, the message speaks loudly to onlookers. "Oh, you've got to be handsome or beautiful or funny or popular to be in this group. I can see I don't really fit here," they conclude either consciously or subconsciously. Including kids who are overweight or of different backgrounds and ethnicity in the up-front part of your program accomplishes more than you might think.

It is through taking responsibility that we actually grow most. Unfortunately, some have never had the opportunity to lead or serve in significant ways simply because of their appearance or personality. Given the opportunity, many of these might be exceptional leaders and servants. The Apostle Paul said those who suffer are actually better able to comfort others, as they can pass on the comfort they have received from God (2 Corinthians 1:4).

People could have debated whether or not I was an outcast during my teenage years. Regardless of how others saw me, I know I often *felt* like an outcast. It was this point when I could have gone either way—positive or negative—that I started attending a local Youth for Christ program and that my youth pastor also began investing in me.

He started encouraging me to use my musical talents by inviting me to use my guitar to lead worship in our junior church program. As an eighth grader, was I ready? Probably not. Was I worthy? No. But serving in that capacity was the best thing for me. It took my eyes off myself and put them onto others. Having the younger kids look up to me boosted my self-esteem as well.

Later that year I sang and played my first solo in church. I was petrified, knowing four hundred people would be focused solely on me. I practiced and practiced. I prayed and prayed. What if my voice cracked or I made a mistake? What if I suddenly lost my place? Would I ever be able to show my face around there again?

When I finished singing, the entire church applauded. They clapped loud and long. I couldn't remember ever having felt so good. I knew that church was a place where I could belong and where God could use me. Certainly, I would have to work through some of those performance issues later in life, but at that time, it was exactly what I needed.

A VICTIM'S PRAYER

One victim of bullying, who came to realize his need to move on with his life, penned this prayer:

> *Lord, please put me to use.*
> *I am filled with fears and, yes, sometimes anger.*
> *As a young bird struggles to fly, I fight to control my hatred toward those*
> *   who have mocked me; yet I know that you hear my pain.*
> *Soothe my pain.*
> *Grant me the same calmness you had when people were plotting against you.*
> *Grant me the strength to forgive.*
> *Help me help others in your name, to the glory of Jesus Christ, the ulti-*
> *   mate example of rising above victimhood.*

reaching the bullies

It is hard to imagine a ministry to fringe kids being complete without an emphasis on reaching bullies. If bullied kids represent those living in Samaria, bullies fit the description just as much. Following Christ demands that we reach out to them as well as to their victims.

In the town where I live, every middle school student is asked the following question as part of their one-to-one orientation: "How do you respond when someone bullies you?"

Answers to this question are very telling. Officials find that kids generally respond in one of three ways. Some start to cry or exhibit other anxious or nervous body language. In this case, educators can assume they have likely been victimized. Others say things like, "What do you mean? Nobody pushes me around!" Usually these kids are doing the bullying. The third response is one of confusion, as these students have obviously never thought of such a question. These are generally the bystanders.

HOW MANY?

What percentage of kids fit into each of these categories? After eliminating bystanders and those only marginally touched by occasional bullying, we are left with those who have been most deeply affected. They fall into three basic categories. First are those victims of bullying who are frequently or severely harassed by their peers and don't fight back. They make up approximately 14 percent of all teenagers. Second are the victims and victimizers—kids who are *both* recipients and perpetrators. They also represent roughly 14 percent of all students. Last are the 16 percent of students who are pure bullies—kids who pick on others but are not picked on themselves.[1]

In total, 30 percent of middle and high school students describe themselves as being bullies! Therefore, to have a balanced ministry to young people, we must have a focus on reaching bullies.

REACHING BULLIES

Just as we must understand the victims of bullying if we are to effectively minister to them, we must also understand what lies behind the actions of bullies if we hope to reach them. Research has shown that there are basic differences between the temperaments of those who bully and those who are victims. For example, German researcher Friedrich Losel discovered that high school bullies had unusually low heart rates (62 beats per minute, compared to the average of 70 beats per minute), indicating a less fearful attitude toward life. Victimized children, on the other hand, had higher heart rates, averaging 75 beats per minute.[2]

There are many reasons kids bully others, but at the forefront are feelings of anger and frustration. For some, the feelings stem from problems at home. Families of those who bully or commit other aggressive acts tend to share at least three common characteristics. First is a sense of disconnection between the family and the rest of society. In other words, the homes they are reared in have a much different value system than the average family, and they tend to remain separate. Second, the parents of these children usually possess inconsistent or permissive attitudes toward aggression and violence. Children with such parents do not learn appropriate self-control or healthy concern for others. And finally, the homes of most bullies are characterized by emotional coldness as well as physical or emotional violence. Such kids understandably become very self-absorbed and focused on fending primarily for themselves.[3]

Youngsters who live with such dysfunction often pick on others in an attempt to gain control over their own lives. Because they sense that their homes are out of control, they look for something or someone to control. They desperately need a place where they belong and feel at home, something biblically functioning youth groups are uniquely positioned to provide. In fact, research has confirmed that children who are involved in such positive activities are far more likely to overcome the above-mentioned obstacles.[4]

While problems at home influence some toward bullying, for others the cause stems more from peer abuse. The abused crosses over to become the abuser when he reaches the point where he can't take any more.

Dr. James Gilligan of the Center for the Study of Violence at Harvard University found vengeance to be the most common theme in the violent acts of the bullied. To the person who feels humiliated, rejected, or ridiculed, violence is an attempt to fight back and even the score. To the person who feels violated, getting revenge is justice, especially when adults have not appropriately intervened. Luke Woodham, the sixteen-year-old who murdered three students in Pearl, Mississippi, said, "I killed because people like me are mistreated every day. My whole life I felt outcast and alone. I finally had to do something about it."[5]

Those children who are both bullies and victims of bullying are the most at risk for having their sadness and anxiety erupt into rage. They behave like bullies through anger and acting out but also experience the depression and anxiety often attributed to victims. It is this oscillation between anxiety and rage that is the most toxic condition of all.

A powerful antidote to this potential horror is unconditional love and acceptance, consistently extended through adults and peers. This releases the power of the Holy Spirit to rescue such kids from suicide, depression, drug abuse, and violence—all to which they are naturally prone.

TWO TYPES OF BULLIES

While bullying behavior may take a myriad of forms, from exclusion to physical brutality, there are generally two different types of bullies behind the abuse, as described below.

Bullies by Influence

This type of bully exercises control and influence over others through charm or competent social skills, enabling him to convince and persuade others to his point of view. These kids are often very popular, with an uncanny ability to bring peers together. Unfortunately, the glue that holds them is their shared energy in picking on or excluding others.

Some of these bullies are driven by anger, others by insecurity. Still others bully because it's all they know. Confronting this type of bully can be very intimidating for a youngster, because every kid fears becoming the next target of the bully's widespread scheme.

Gary, a junior high classmate of mine, was extremely athletic and possessed a quick wit. Many were attracted to him, but he also had a dark, cruel streak in him. He and his followers regularly preyed on certain "weak" targets. Though his followers would not have normally picked on such kids, in Gary's shadow they became brutal and obnoxious.

Bullies by Force

Even as a sixth grader, Chuck weighed close to two hundred pounds, making him the king of any middle school hill. Unlike Gary, he was not a popular kid, but who was going to argue with him?

For reasons still unknown to me, Chuck found great pleasure in picking on me. Perhaps it was because I was the new kid in a small school where few new students came and went from year to year. I could bet on getting slammed against a bathroom stall, having my arm cranked behind my back in the hallway, or being sat on during recess until I said a thousand "uncles" or whatever phrase he might demand of me.

I was just grateful I could run faster than Chuck, and that he didn't ride my school bus, making the torturous day that much longer. Much of my sixth grade year was consumed with making sure I wasn't in the same general vicinity as he. To the best of my recollection, no teacher, principal, or fellow student ever stood up for me or confronted Chuck, nor did I expect them to. We all believed that such horrors were just an inescapable part of the madness of middle school life.

Kids like Gary and Chuck need to be confronted, but most kids are just grateful not to be one of their victims. Confronting is the furthest thing from their minds. However, following is a process for effective confrontation for those with enough courage to do so.

1. Initiate the confrontation through the relationship of a caring adult. In most cases, adults need to develop meaningful relationships with bullies if there is to be a breakthrough with them. Obviously, it is wonderful when fellow teenagers have the respect and confidence to directly confront bullies, but that is rare.

Once a solid relationship is established, a caring adult is in a prime position to confront bullying behavior. Even then, it must be done respectfully. Point out the influence that the bully has and the good he or she is capable of, assuming that the bully would want to lead for good and not evil.

2. Make every effort to understand them. Years after high school I learned that Gary had grown up in an abusive home. Carrying an enormous amount of internal rage, he used his natural gifts to channel his anger toward others negatively. Because Gary had so many natural abilities, nobody would have guessed he had such problems. Had someone recognized his bullying as evidence of a deeper problem, life might have been much easier for a lot of kids, including Gary.

In the same way, Chuck was also a very insecure boy. His size and weight made him a natural outcast. To compensate for his vulnerability, he became the tough kid, putting fear into the hearts of his peers. And though he wasn't popular, at least he wasn't picked on. My plight was a constant reminder to everyone of just how miserable Chuck could make someone's life. Again, what if someone had been willing to see through that "tough guy" facade and minister to the heart of a lonely, hurting boy? I know life would have been a whole lot less agonizing for me.

3. Apply gentle but consistent consequences. Bullies can only survive when the silent majority lets them act with impunity. Every school, youth group, or family must create an atmosphere that says, "Nobody hurts another person here." Speaking up to stop bullying is not tattling. Rather, it is an act of maturity and courage.

When teasing is clearly meant to belittle and includes threats, or the interchange is highly emotionally charged, it is important to apply gentle consequences, with "gentle" being the operative word. Overly harsh or degrading discipline only causes humiliation and embarrassment. It also forces the rest of the group to choose between you (the leader) and one of their peers. They may have psychologically aligned themselves with you. Yet if you react inappropriately or degrade even a bully, the others will side with their peer at your expense every time. Kids should always be handled respectfully and calmly.

Young people do not mind having their behavior corrected as long as, in the process, they are left with their dignity firmly intact. The following list of gentle corrections are designed to do just that.

1. Speak to the young person privately to review the group's commitment to treat one another with dignity. Come to an agreement on a plan with a commitment to follow it.

2. Have the young person sit out from a preferred activity.

3. If consistent violations continue, a written plan may need to be developed to deal with the harassment and abuse of fellow members.

4. As a last resort, enforce a minimal respite from group activities, with a warm welcome back when the period is completed. How many times should they be invited back? How about seventy times seven?

5. Speak with the offender about the importance of apologizing to the violated member or members of the group so that reconciliation can occur.

4. Emphasize the natural consequences of bullying. A wise person once said, "No one will change until the pain of staying the same becomes greater than the pain of changing." This is certainly true with bullies. Helping them realize some of the negative results of their behavior makes them much more willing to embrace change.

Many aggressive children do not consciously consider the ramifications of their actions. Help them think through the consequences. They may come up with such things as:

1. I lose friends when I lose my temper.

2. I get into trouble when I pick on other kids.

3. Adults I respect and want to please are disappointed when I pick on others.

4. I don't get invited to things I would like to attend.

5. Bullying is habit-forming. As a result, I have trouble making and keeping friends.

6. Others have been truly hurt by my teasing and bullying.

7. Bullying often leads to other forms of trouble. (Bullies are six times more likely to end up as juvenile delinquents.)

5. Move them toward biblical atonement. To atone means "to make amends for." Just like victims need to forgive, perpetrators need opportunities to make atonement to those they have wronged.

Of the thirty boys out of jail who have lived with us in our home, those who were able to seek forgiveness and make amends have fared best. Many think that kids who commit violent acts are heartless and void of a conscience, but we have actually found the opposite true. Most ruthless acts of violence are motivated by feelings of shame, worthlessness, and despair. When given the opportunity to make amends, new life is breathed into these kids. One of the boys who lived with us explained his situation:

"I couldn't sleep at all the night before I was supposed to meet with Josh's family, the kid I had hurt. I was bracing for lots of hatred and revenge from them because of what I had done. But I still wanted to meet with them because it weighed so heavy on me every day. On the streets I just smoked weed to forget all that stuff, but now I wanted to start handling it different. When his mom told me she forgave me, I couldn't believe it. It felt like a thousand pounds came off my shoulders. And it made me want to never hurt another person as long as I lived."

6. Entrust them to lead. Many bullies are effective leaders of at least some peers, albeit negative leaders. Our job is to provide them with positive opportunities to exercise their gifts. Some schools in Norway have actually been very effective at placing former bullies in the role of big brothers and sisters to new children who enter their classes. The same strategies can be used in youth groups.

I've found it best to handle troubled kids by first acknowledging their abilities. Tell them how much they are needed, especially in helping some of the less fortunate ones. Most of them are longing for the chance to prove to themselves and others that they can become agents for good. When we give responsibilities to the biggest troublemakers, nine out of ten times they rise to our level of expectations.

Short of this, we're only focusing on the negative traits in the young person's life. But eliminating bad things from someone's life, without replacing them with something good, merely leaves a person empty. And no one will stay empty for long. They'll fill the void with all sorts of things. By calling kids to accept godly responsibilities, we are not simply telling them what to say "no" to, we are giving them something to say "yes" to. Anything short of that amounts to little more than training in "sin management."

In videotapes made just hours before the Columbine massacre, Eric Harris and Dylan Klebold declared, "We're going to kick-start a revolution—a revolution of the dispossessed." Promising to live forever in the memories and nightmares of all those who had made them feel like nobodies, they were fantasizing about creating a cult filled with those who had suffered and been cast out. Out of a twisted sense of purpose and martyrdom they envisioned movie directors fighting over their story.[6] When we fail to help kids gain a sense of their God-given purpose, they will surely find something else to replace it.

7. Know when to refer. Experts agree that bullies need help in being able to empathize with their victims, a skill that doesn't come naturally for most of them. Victims, on the other hand, need emotional first aid. At times this can be accomplished through caring adults who are willing to listen, empathize, and teach simple social skills. At other times, youngsters may require special attention from counselors.

Generally, whenever youth are involved with gangs, drugs, cultic activities, or other potentially dangerous behavior, outside referrals are recommended. Depressed or suicidal teens and those with apparent mental illness also require immediate attention. Whenever outside professional help is called upon, parental permission *must* be obtained.

Just a further word about mental illness, as it can be a significant factor in anti-social behavior. It has become more and more clear just how much chemical imbalances in the brain can affect behavior. In serious cases of attention-deficit disorder, compulsive disorders, or bipolar disorders medical help and medication is essential. If we ignore this reality, using only the methods previously mentioned, we do kids a great disservice. It is similar to telling a diabetic to modify her behavior rather than take insulin.

Inviting counselors, social workers, psychologists, or psychiatrists to provide training for staff and volunteers on topics like addictions, abuse, mental illness, and emotional disorders would increase the effectiveness of any youth program. Having a relationship with such professionals is also important so that you know who to call when the crises arise. We can get into serious trouble when we operate outside the realm in which we are trained and qualified.

FOR SUCH A TIME AS THIS?

The Columbine school killings signaled a watershed event in contemporary youth culture. Eighteen-year-old Heather Miller explained to Time magazine how that event changed her life forever. "A lot of martyrs have been older, but now we're hearing about teens doing it."

Columbine student Dana Scott, sister of the martyred Rachel Scott said, "It is in our hands right now as a young generation. We've been put in this position, and I think God is raising up a generation that is going to do things differently."[7]

A scene during the 1999 massacre of Christian youth in a Fort Worth prayer meeting offers another glimpse into what God is doing in today's young people. Nineteen-year-old Jeremiah Neitz, himself a former outcast and fringe kid, stood up in the midst of the shooting in his church sanctuary and walked up to the man who had just murdered seven people. Jeremiah's youth leader, lying on the floor, pulled desperately on his pant leg, begging him to duck down.

Jeremiah continued anyway, and as he reached the shooter, the befuddled man leveled his gun at Jeremiah's head. "Sir, you can shoot me if you want," Jeremiah responded, "I know where I'm going—I'm going to heaven. What you need is Jesus Christ in your life."

The gunman turned away, put the gun to his own head, and fired.[8]

Hold that scene for a moment. It may be prophetic. Many of our youth are ready to rise and take steps of faith that could well cost them their lives. I believe this generation is looking for a cause big enough to die for. If we don't give it to them, surely another cause will capture them.

Today's teenagers are not coming to our youth groups just to play silly games or to hear nice sermonettes. They want to sink their teeth into something much bigger. The question is, "Are *we* up to the challenge?" We cannot lead our youth farther than we have gone ourselves.

Some of today's teenagers remind me of a pastor I met in 1984 when I was smuggling Bibles into Communist China. He had just been released after several years of imprisonment for teaching about Jesus Christ. I had the privilege of meeting him at an early morning prayer meeting he was leading. Afterward I asked him what prison was like in China, anxious to hear a firsthand account of the gruesome details. His only response was, "God has been very good to me."

This man became a hero to me. I had heard of how the authorities had threatened to burn his house and all that he owned if he started meeting with Christians again. His response: "I consider everything a loss compared to the surpassing greatness of knowing Christ."

Then they threatened to put him back in prison permanently. To that he replied, "Nothing can separate me from the love of God that is in Christ Jesus."

Finally, they vowed to take his life if he didn't cease his underground activities. "For me to live is Christ, and to die is gain," was his response.

It is no wonder the Chinese authorities feared this man. They couldn't afford to keep him in prison, for people around him were coming to vibrant faith left and right. And they couldn't risk killing him for fear that his death might only further the growth of the church. The early church father, Tertullian, declared as much in the third century, "Blood of the martyrs is the seed of the church." Jesus said it another way, "Unless a kernel of wheat falls to the ground and dies, it remains only a single seed. But if it dies, it produces many" (John 12:24).

Revival always has a cost. Could it be that these seeds of revival and self-sacrifice are being planted in America today? And might they be sprouting in our young people? Might they be ready to commit their lives to radically serving others, even the unlovely and unlovable? Perhaps our wildest prayers are being answered before our very eyes.

Truly, this generation of youth is unusual. They appear much more willing to sell out for Jesus than many of those before them. Many are ready for the challenge to boldly venture into Samaria. We must be there to train, equip, and lead by example—fanning into flame the sparks God has kindled in their young lives. Let us point them to Jerusalem, to Judea, to Samaria, and then to the ends of the earth.

APPENDIX 1

reaching fringe kids

A SIX-SESSION COURSE FOR YOUTH GROUPS

tips for leaders

Time and Place

The following sessions can be used in a variety of settings, such as a youth group program or in a Sunday school class. You will need approximately sixty to ninety minutes to complete each session.

Session Objectives

We want the kids to feel in depth what it's like to be an outcast, to be bullied, and to be a bully, if they have not already done so. If they have experienced these things, the sessions should help them learn ways to effectively handle them.

We also expect your kids to feel God's call on their lives to reach out to their hurting peers and learn effective ways to do so.

Note: *The sessions are not for preaching or Bible study. Rather, they are designed to facilitate experiential learning through activities, stories, and Bible passages.*

Leader Sharing

During each session, it is good for the leader to share a brief personal experience on the topic being discussed. This will help to create identity and credibility with youth. But remember, *most* of the sharing and discussion should come from the young people.

Scripture Readings

Use an easy-to-understand Bible translation. Read dramatically with expression. You might have a good reader alternate the reading with you, or have two good readers alternate reading.

When you read long passages, it is likely that kids will lose interest and not pay close attention, so it's very important to use a conversational Bible translation and to read well.

You may find it helpful to print out the passages and pass them out for youth to follow along. This will ensure that everyone has the same translation. And it prevents newcomers from being embarrassed when they don't know how to find things.

Reviews and Closings

After the first session, we suggest having a review session each week. This will help to reinforce the learning and activities and will tell you what the youth are feeling and experiencing. It will also inform those who were absent.

Of course, you'll *never* want to say, "Class, let's review." Instead, conduct creative reviews such as those described below.

TOSSING — Toss out something fun, such as a Koosh ball, Nerf ball, Beanie Baby, or stuffed animal. Ask whoever catches it to tell one thing he or she remembers from last week (or ask for a more specific response). After a person responds, he or she tosses the item to another person, who does the same.

Or you can first ask a specific question about a previous session. Then toss out the object. Those who catch it may answer the question or toss it on.

Note: *Never embarrass anyone who is shy or reluctant. Always say that responding is optional. Say, "If you want to share do so. If you want to wait, toss it to someone else." You don't want them to dread this activity.*

After several people have shared, you can take the object back. Then ask if anyone else can tell something he or she remembers or has a comment to express.

SUBGROUPS — You can divide the group into pairs or groups of threes or fours. Ask each subgroup to take five or ten minutes to list what they can remember from last week. Then ask for a representative from each subgroup to report to the whole group.

ILLUSTRATIONS — Divide the group into pairs or groups of threes or fours. Give each group large sheets of paper (poster board, flip-chart page, or newsprint paper) and markers. Ask them to draw depictions of what they remember from the last session. Then ask for a representative to explain their drawing to the whole group. Affix the drawings to the wall, and keep them on display throughout the series.

SONGS, RAPS, POEMS, OR SKITS — Form groups of four to six people. Ask each group to develop a song, rap, reading, poem, or skit about the previous session. If you sense they have problems doing this, suggest that they make a list or drawing. This activity can be very successful and a lot of fun, but the youth need to feel comfortable in the group to effectively participate.

In addition to reviews, closings can be a meaningful time to hear from the students. You could use any of the above methods to have the kids tell any of the following:

- What they found significant about the session
- What questions they have about the session
- What comments they want to make about the session

Permission to Photocopy

At times during these sessions, you are asked to photocopy specific sections of the book for kids to read or use in activities.

Permission to photocopy the specified sections from *Risk in Our Midst* is granted for local church use only. Copyright © Scott Larson. Published by Group Publishing, Inc., P.O. Box 481, Loveland, CO 80539.

feeling like an outcast

Purpose

To have kids experience and understand how it feels to be an outcast

Opening Activity

Select one young person who is secure and articulate, but do not tell that person you have chosen him or her. Prep several of that student's closest friends just before the meeting so they can help you. When the meeting starts, they should purposely ignore, move away from, or avoid eye contact with their friend in a way that is obvious to the entire group. Don't let this go very long, causing the person to feel overly embarrassed or humiliated.

Opening Discussion

Say: **Today we are going to talk about what it feels like to be excluded.**

Explain to the group how one person was set up to make a point. Then ask the group these questions:

• **What are some of the things that made him (or her) feel excluded?**

• **What are some other things that make people feel excluded?**

Ask the excluded person:

• **What did this feel like to you?**

• **What was going on in your mind?**

• **How did you feel about your friends?**

• **How did it make you feel about yourself?**

Ask the entire group:

• **Can any of you think of a time when you had some of these same feelings? Explain the situation and how it affected you.** (As the leader, also give an example from your own life.)

• **What are some reasons people exclude others?**

• **Can you think of a time when you were part of a group that excluded others?**
• **What were the reasons you did it?**

Story

Tell the group the story about Brian in Chapter 1, page 10, or have a couple of good readers take turns reading parts of the story. Be sure to include his poem.

Ask the entire group:
• **What is your initial reaction to this story? Explain.**
• **How does this story challenge you?**

Scripture

After the story, say: **Now we'll look at a man in the Bible who was also excluded by others.** Read aloud the story of Zacchaeus in Luke 19:1-10. For added creativity, have kids work together to create an improvisational skit based on this Scripture passage. Or have two good readers take turns reading the passage while other kids silently act out the story. Make sure all the students have a Bible so they can follow the reading.

After exploring the Bible story, lead kids in a brief discussion. Ask:
• **Why didn't people accept Zacchaeus?**
• **How well do you think people knew him before passing judgment?**
• **How would you have felt about yourself if you were he?**
• **How would you have felt about the others?**
• **How do you think Zacchaeus felt going into that crowd?**
• **Why do you think Jesus went to his house knowing how unpopular that decision would be?**
• **Why do you think Zacchaeus responded so radically?**
• **Who do you see yourself most like: Zacchaeus or the crowd? Explain.**

Closing

If there is time, ask the following questions. You may want to use some of the closing activities mentioned in "Tips for Leaders" at the beginning of Appendix 1 (p. 118).
• **What was important to you about this session?**
• **What questions do you have about it?**
• **What comments do you have about the session?**

Survey

Say: **Before we close, please fill out a survey on our youth group.** Give each person a pen and a copy of the Youth Group Climate Survey 1—For Youth in Appendix 2 (pp. 145-146). Have kids complete their surveys then return them to you. At the same time have youth leaders complete the Youth Group Climate Survey for Adult Leaders in Appendix 2 (pp. 143-144) and return them unless you meet with leaders separately to take the survey.

Close by saying: **For the next four weeks, one of the things we will discuss is how to improve our youth group climate.**

The curse of any adult or teenager is to feel left out—like we just don't fit in. We have all felt like outsiders from time to time. So you'd think we'd be a bit more sensitive to those who receive more than their share of exclusion. Unfortunately, that is not the case.

Excluding someone is wrong: both when we do it as well as when others do it. Ironically, Jesus went out of his way to meet excluded people. And he received great responses from them. Let's pray that we will follow his example.

Close with prayer. [Sometime in next week's lesson, have group members take Youth Group Climate Survey 2—For Youth, also in Appendix 2 (p. 147).]

a welcoming environment

Purpose

To help kids recognize and overcome favoritism in the group

Opening Activity

Before the discussion, have chairs set up in different configurations throughout the room. Make sure you have at least as many chairs as the number of kids you are expecting. Each chair should have a number on it.

Some of the chairs should be alone. Some should be facing the walls. Some may be just outside the door of the room you're meeting in. Put several together in a large circle, then make two or three smaller circles as well. Put a few of them up higher on top of something.

As kids come in, randomly hand them each a number and ask them to find the chair with the number and sit in it.

Opening Discussion

Once kids are seated say: **Tonight we are going to talk about how we treat people who come to our youth group. Most of us treat some people better than others. We have our favorites or those we prefer. We don't treat everyone with the same respect and concern.**

We have arranged the chairs to show some of the different ways we treat people. They show how we are more accepting of some than others. And how we even exclude some people.

Have kids explain how the chair arrangements represent the different ways kids might treat people in the group. Then ask:

- **Are there any others that we might have missed?**
- **Have any of you felt like you were sitting in one of these seats? Where and when?** (If the kids are slow to respond, give an example from your life.)
- **How would you describe our youth group? How would you**

set up the room to accurately show that?

• **Where do you think a newcomer would feel that he or she is seated?**

• **What would make him or her feel like a member of the group?**

• **What grade would you give our group on accepting others? Explain.**

• **What could we do to be more accepting?** (Here you can talk about the results of the previous week's survey.)

Scripture

Read aloud James 2:1-5. Use an easy-to-understand Bible translation. Read dramatically with expression. You might have a good reader alternate the reading with you, or have two good readers alternate reading. Then discuss these questions:

• **What kinds of kids do we tend to quickly put in the center of our group?**

• **What kinds of kids do we tend to seat outside either directly or indirectly?**

• **Treating some people better than others is called favoritism. Why do you think we show favoritism?**

• **How does God look upon favoritism?**

• **When has favoritism hurt you?**

• **When have you personally shown favoritism?**

Say: **Research confirms that 48 percent of students believe that associating with students of a lower level would result in the reduction of their own social status as well.**

Ask:

• **Do you think that is true for us? for you individually? Why or why not?**

• **As a group, do you think we can stop showing favoritism? If so, what would it take?**

Story

The following story is about a youth group where newcomers are welcomed and treated with respect and love—a youth group where favoritism is not shown.

Ginny brought her thirteen-year-old friend Jamie to her youth group. A couple of days later Ginny received the following note:

Your youth group is great! It's fun and it helped me get more in touch with God. I was never really involved in religion before, but I felt very comfortable. It's the only place I've ever been where everyone is popular. Thanks for taking me. Now I realize what a true friend you are.

Ginny explained, "This was Jamie's first time at any youth group meeting so he was a little nervous. He doesn't really have any friends at school. Kids think he's gay because of how he dresses."

After reading the story, ask:

• **Would someone like Jamie feel this way about our group? Would he be able to say that our group is a place where everyone is popular? Why or why not?**

Review

Check the "Tips for Leaders" section (p. 118) for some ideas for a creative review.

Say: **Last week we talked about feeling excluded.**

Ask: • **What do you remember about last week?**

• **Remember Brian? Who can tell us about him?**

• **Would Brian have felt included in our youth group? Why or why not?**

• **Do you believe that his acceptance by a youth group might have saved his life?**

Closing

If there is time, ask the following questions. You may want to use some of the methods mentioned in "Tips for Leaders" (p. 118).

• **What was important to you about this session?**

• **What questions do you have about it?**

• **What comments do you have about the session?**

Close by saying: **We all naturally fall into the trap of favoritism and excluding others like Brian and Jamie, kids who are excluded by most other kids. Yet there were few things Jesus confronted so strongly. In Matthew 25, Jesus says that how we treat those considered "the least" among us is how we treat him.**

Any sort of change demands serious self-examination, repentance, and a commitment to live otherwise.

Let's take a few minutes to be silent before God right now. Let's examine our own hearts and talk with God about it.

Close with a few minutes of silent prayer. Consider having students complete Youth Group Climate Survey 2—For Youth, in Appendix 2 (p. 147).

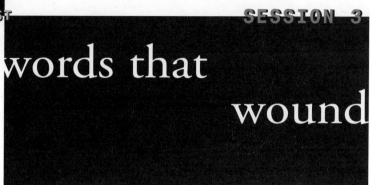

Purpose

To have kids recognize the power of words to hurt and then avoid them

Opening Activity

Bring a large box with "Danger: Wild Animal" written in large, bold letters on the top and all sides. If possible, get an appliance box and cover it with paper such as blank newsprint.

Place the box where kids can see it as they enter. If possible, have a recording of animal sounds playing. If the box is large enough, you could have someone inside growling, making noises, and thumping the box around.

As you begin the meeting, build suspense by telling the kids that you have brought in the wildest, most dangerous animal known. Ask them what animal they think is the wildest, one that cannot be tamed by any person.

After hearing several responses, say that you are going to show them the wildest thing there is. Again build suspense by saying: **Watch out! I'm going to open the box. The faint-hearted should close their eyes. Hold onto someone strong. Are you ready?** Then, open the box. Reach inside, and pull out a large red tongue. (You can create the tongue by sewing two pieces of red felt together, then stuffing it with paper. Or, if you prefer, you can simply use poster board and markers to create a large picture of a tongue.)

Opening Discussion

Ask kids why they think the tongue would be in there. Then have someone read aloud James 3:7-8. Ask:

- **Why does the Bible say that the tongue is so hard to tame?**
- **Do you ever have a hard time controlling your tongue? Explain.**

• **Which is harder for you to control, your actions or your words? Why?**

• **What do you think of the saying, "Sticks and stones may break my bones but words can never hurt me"?**

Say: **James 3:8 says that our tongues are evil and spread deadly poison. Listen to this example, a note that eight-year-old Wanda handed to another girl in school:**

> *Awful Janet*
> *Your the stinkiest girl in this world. I hope you die but of course I suppose that's impossible. I've got some ideas:*
> *1. Play in the road*
> *2. Cut your throad*
> *3. Drink poison*
> *4. get drunk*
> *5. knife yourself*
> *Please do some of this you big fat Girl. we all hate you. I'm praying Oh please lord let Janet die. Were in need of fresh air. Did you hear me lord cause if you didn't will all die with her here. See Janet we're not all bad.*
> *From Wanda Jackson*[1]

Continue with the discussion by asking:

• **Which hurts worse, to be physically hurt or to be hurt by someone's words? Explain.**

• **Which heals faster? Explain.**

• **How have you been hurt by words?**

• **Can you think of a time when you have hurt someone with your words?**

• **Why do people attack others with what they say?**

• **What are some different ways to attack verbally?** (If kids are slow to respond, offer these suggestions—gossip, accusations, name-calling, talking behind your back, and sarcasm.)

Scripture

Read aloud James 3:1-12. Remember to use an easy-to-understand Bible translation. Read dramatically with expression. You might have a good reader alternate the reading with you, or have two good readers alternate reading. After the reading, discuss these questions with the group:

• **How is the tongue like a horse's bit or a ship's rudder?**

- **How is it like a spark that sets a forest on fire?**
- **How is it possible that good and encouraging words come out of the same mouth as bad and negative words?**
- **What would help us to have more positive than negative things come out?**
- **How do you think God can help us with this?**

Closing

If there is time, ask the following questions. You may want to use some of the methods mentioned in "Tips for Leaders" (p. 118).

- **What was important to you about this session?**
- **What questions do you have about it?**
- **What comments do you have about the session?**

Close by saying: **The Bible says that no *person* can tame the tongue. That is why we really need God's help with that. The more we are filled with him on the inside, the more good things will flow out.**

If you have hurt others with words, you need to ask forgiveness and help to make amends. If you have been hurt by words, ask God to heal you and help you to forgive the one or ones who have hurt you.

If you haven't invited God into your life, that is where you need to start. He will begin changing you on the inside. If you already have a relationship with him, the more time you spend with him, reading the Bible and praying, the more you will be filled with his goodness.

Next week we are going to talk more about the power of words. We will discuss how we can know when harmless teasing crosses the line into harmful bullying.

Close with prayer. If you think it's appropriate, allow time for kids to go to others in the group and ask forgiveness for hurtful words they have said.

phrases, frames, and unwholesome talk

Purpose

To have kids identify and curb unwholesome talk using a pictorial example

Opening Review

Begin this week with a creative review of weeks 1-3. You might want to use one or more of the methods described in "Tips for Leaders" at the beginning of this appendix (p. 118).

Opening Discussion

After the review, say: **Last week we began discussing the role of words and how cruel kids can be. Do you remember the note Wanda wrote to Janet?** (You might read parts of the note again.) **It's clear to anyone that these are very hurtful words. Most of us would not hurt people with words like that, but most of us do use hurtful words with others sometimes. It's just more subtle, and we're not often aware of it.**

This session will help us become more aware of words that may not seem hurtful on the surface but still hurt.

Scripture

Read aloud Ephesians 4:29. Then ask:

- **How would you describe unwholesome talk?**
- **Do you think teasing is unwholesome?**
- **How about sarcasm?**

Say: **Much of the fun we have with one another is a result of our use of humor. We don't want to completely eliminate kidding around or harmless sarcasm.**

Ask: • **How do we know when we cross over the line and sarcasm,**

teasing, and humor becomes bullying?
* **What about gossip? How is that unwholesome talk?**

Story

Say: **Scott Larson, author of this series, recalls a camp he attended while in middle school. Listen to how he describes his experience:**

"**Typical of boys' cabins, our conversation was filled with crude sarcasm, brutal put-downs, and degrading comments about the girls at camp. What made it so unusual, though, was the presence of our classmate, Chip. It wasn't what Chip said, but what he didn't say that was so profound.**

"**Though he never confronted us, he was noticeably silent when it came to participating. The thing that stands out in my mind years later is how his silence changed the climate of our cabin. By the end of the week, the gossip and harsh jokes had literally ceased, which I contribute solely to Chip's influence.**"

After reading the story, ask:

* **How would you describe the "verbal climate" of our youth group?**

* **How could we improve our "verbal climate" as a group?**

Frames and Phrases

Lead kids through a discussion of the material in Chapter 6, pages 58 to 64. Use the visual illustration (explained in Chapter 6) to help explain the concepts to kids. For example, you could draw a picture frame on a flip-chart or transparency as you talk.

Say: **The image of a picture frame can be helpful to understand when harmless sarcasm, teasing, and humor turn into bullying. When two people are within the borders of a picture frame together, their relationship is secure enough to withstand teasing and sarcasm. However, when one person is outside the frame, confusion and hurt feelings can easily result.**

Think about some things that make it difficult for people to exist in the same frame.

List kids' responses on your flip-chart or transparency. Include the list from Chapter 6 (pp. 59-60)—different genders, racial and ethnic boundaries, audience, personality issues, and having a bad day.

Say: **Now let's think about some rules we might create concerning how words or phrases are used. I'll list a few to start us off, and then we can add more to the list:**

1. **NEVER tease about physical characteristics (nose, weight, hair).**
2. **NEVER tease about things you suspect someone might be sensitive about (glasses, complexion, family issues).**
3. **NEVER use humor or teasing as a way to get back at people.**
4. **NEVER label kids with degrading names like "Fatso," "Beanpole," "Nerd," "Geek," "Stupid," and so on. What are some other names you can think of?**
5. **NEVER make degrading comparisons to objects or animals (excrement, cow, dog).**
6. **NEVER say things publicly that you learned in private, breaking confidentiality.**

Allow kids to add any additional rules they wish.

Discussion

When the list is complete, say: **By far, teasing is the most common type of verbal bullying by youth of all ages. Many perceive the verbal harassment they receive as being just as threatening as physical attacks.**

There seems to be a lot of confusion for both teens and adults when it comes to teasing. For example, an overwhelming majority of teenagers believe that most teasing is "done in fun, not to hurt others." But, on the other hand, that same majority defined teasing as bullying and reported feeling traumatized by it.

The confusion is understandable, for even the word "tease" has two completely different definitions. One is "to playfully fool around," while the other is "to annoy or harass by persistent mocking or poking fun."

During a focus panel with a group of eleventh graders in a small Christian school, one young man confessed, "We tease each other a lot here, and sometimes I wonder if I may be hurting someone's feelings. I guess I'm not sure how to tell if I am."

As they brainstormed ways to deal with this issue, many positive ideas developed. One was simply to respectfully ask whether the teasing was becoming hurtful. Another was to watch for defensive body language or other signs that an individual was disengaging from the group.

Just as the conversation was wrapping up, one girl stood up and in a loud but tremulous voice, said, "You guys have teased me about my weight since I was in the third grade. I hated it then and

I hate it now!" As she was speaking, her classmates' faces expressed both shock and horror.

Group Projects

Form groups of four to six people. Assign each group one of the following projects:

1. Develop a role-play or skit where someone is using one of these hurtfully: teasing, being sarcastic, gossip, or using humor.

2. Practice one of the first three skits in Appendix 3 (p. 149). Encourage kids to improvise and change the skits as they wish, making them as realistic as possible.

Allow about fifteen minutes for groups to complete their assignments. When assignments have been completed, have each group present to the entire group.

After each presentation, ask questions such as:

- **How did this presentation make you feel?**
- **Have you ever had an experience like that? Explain.**
- **How do you think the unwholesome words affected the victim?**
- **What did you learn from this?**

Closing

If there is time, ask the following questions. You may want to use some of the methods mentioned in "Tips for Leaders" at the beginning of this appendix (p. 118).

- **What was important to you about this session?**
- **What questions do you have about it?**
- **What comments do you have about the session?**

Close by saying: **Words have tremendous power to both harm and heal us. We've all been wounded by words and we carry those words with us to this day. Some of us may have even wounded others in such a way, but don't realize it. That's why the Bible talks so much about not letting any unwholesome talk come from our mouths.**

Because our society is so filled with negative talk and humor, most of us just fall into the same patterns. That's what makes kids like Chip stand out so much. Are you willing to be a force for good like he was?

Let's pray and ask God to take control of our tongues this week. Close with prayer.

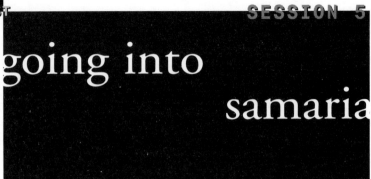

going into
samaria

Purpose

To help kids understand the ways their interactions affect others

Opening Activity

Make two large paper cutouts (twelve to fifteen inches long) and name them "John Paper Boy" and "Jane Paper Girl." Begin the session by saying you want to introduce the group to some friends of yours. Show them the cutouts of "John Paper Boy" and "Jane Paper Girl."

Tell them that you are going to give each person in the room an opportunity to leave their marks on John and Jane. They can write on them, tear them, fold them, or do whatever they want. Start one in the front row and one in the back row.

Each person should take only one or two seconds to do something unique to the cutout, then pass it on. Keep the cutouts moving fast, and then collect them. They will likely be written on, spit on, have gum on them, and have missing limbs.

Bring them to the front to display. Say: **Wow, these paper people were my friends. Look what you did to them! You guys sure are hard on people!**

Opening Discussion

Say: **Every person we meet contributes something to our lives. Some of it is good, and some is bad. Sometimes they add things** (point to gum, ink, and so on), **and sometimes they take things away** (point to any holes or missing limbs). **But we're all changed as a result.**

Ask:

• **What groups of kids in your school have been most damaged by the negative contributions of others?**

• **What group of kids in your school has harmed you the most? helped you the most?**

Scripture

Read aloud Acts 1:8.

Draw three large concentric circles on a large sheet of poster board, flip-chart paper, or newsprint. Inside the inner circle, write "Jerusalem." In the middle circle, write "Judea," and in the outer circle write "Samaria." Be sure to leave space in each circle so you can add comments made by the kids. Outside the outer circle, write "the ends of the earth."

Explain that Jerusalem represents our family and the friends we meet every day. Ask the group to yell out some of these names. You may need to start this. Then write some of the names in the area marked "Jerusalem."

Judea represents a wider context—those "potential friends" around us who we see regularly but don't really know. Many of these people may have special needs that we can recognize. Ask the group to name some of these people. Write down those names in the area marked "Judea." If kids have trouble thinking of folks to include in this section, you might suggest the homeless, shut-ins at the nursing home, children living in a nearby orphanage, younger kids in the church, acquaintances at school, and so on.

The ends of the earth represents the exciting two-week mission trips to Guatemala or Haiti. But Samaria represents the outcasts in our midst. Ask kids what groups might represent Samaria to them? Again, write on the area marked "Samaria" the groups kids suggest.

Say: **Although Samaria is close to home, we avoid it like the plague. It's that section of the cafeteria where someone sits isolated and alone. It's the front seat of the school bus where spitwads and rubber bands are routinely aimed.**

Tell the story about Stringbean in Chapter 9, page 98, where Scott Larson, author of this book, visited "Samaria" and it changed his life. You could ask one or two of the kids to tell or read this story. Give them a copy of it a week before this session. If someone tells the story, add any important points missed.

After reading the story, say: **Samaria is also the back row of a classroom where girls are badgered and mocked about their physical appearance and the athletic field where boys are made fun of because of inferior skills. Just as in Jesus' day, it's the area so-called good people try hard to avoid.**

Skit

Make seven copies of the skit, *Jesus Went to Samaria* (p. 153), and assign the parts. For the skit, you'll need four boys, one girl, and one reader. If possible, distribute copies of the skit a week in advance so kids can practice. Suggest that the kids wear costumes and use props. Always have extra copies in case some get lost or kids are absent.

Have the actors present the skit for the whole group.

Scripture

After the play, read aloud John 4:1-18. Then ask:

• **Why do you think Jesus felt compelled to go through Samaria when every other Jew carefully avoided it, going way around?**

• **What do verses 6-9 and 17-18 tell us about how this woman was treated and how she felt about herself?** (If kids have trouble coming up with ideas, you might suggest these: She came to the well at high noon when no others would be there. She was surprised that a Jewish man would speak to her. Jews would be considered ceremonially unclean by touching a vessel handled by a Samaritan. She had committed adultery; Jews could stone her to death for that.)

• **What are some ways Jesus broke cultural barriers to reach out to her?** (Again, if kids have trouble, offer these suggestions: He was in Samaria. He came to the well at noon when the average person wouldn't. He spoke to a woman, something not culturally acceptable in that day. He asked her for help. He engaged someone in conversation that everyone else would have avoided.)

• **How do you think Jesus' actions might have affected the disciples' view of Samaritans?**

Give each person an index card and a pen. Say: **On your cards, write the names of two or three kids in your school who are treated like despised Samaritans. Then, on the back of your card, write one or two things you could do this week to begin breaking down barriers and reaching out to them.**

When kids have finished, ask:

• **What things could you do to influence others in your school to be more sensitive to them?**

• **How do you think our youth group would respond if "Samaritan" kids started attending?**

• **How do you wish we would respond to "Samaritans" in our midst?**

Say: **It's always easier to reach out to people in Jerusalem, Judea, or the ends of the earth. But Jesus commands us to go into Samaria as well. In fact, it was here that some of his most fruitful ministry occurred. John mentions that within only a couple of days after Jesus' encounter with the Samaritan woman, a great number of people believed because of her faith.**

Samaritans—or outcasts—represent the heart of God. In the New Testament, Jesus actively seeks out at least five distinct types of people: the poor, the sick, the orphan, the widow, and the imprisoned. In one way or another, they are all outcasts, Samaritans.

Letter to Newsweek Magazine

Say: **Listen to the challenge given by a seventeen-year-old girl in a recent "Letter to the Editor" of Newsweek magazine:**

> *"Think about the average American high school. Think about the groups. The cliques. Now think about the students who are not in a group, not in a clique. The outsiders, the freaks, the weirdos, the geeks. To all my fellow students who may be reading this: you could prevent another tragedy from happening in your own seemingly safe school. Say hello to the guy who sits alone in chemistry and never speaks. Invite someone who always sits by herself at lunch to sit with you.*
>
> *"Think about what you are doing when you tease, laugh at, or exclude someone from something just because he doesn't fit in. This may not solve the problem; some people are just not mentally stable. But if the youth in our schools make an effort to stop ostracizing such students, schools might become safer places. Maybe even happier, too."[2]*

Close by saying: **Let's pray that we will accept the challenge expressed in that letter. Let us ask God to help us reach out to students who need our love.**

Close with prayer.

acting it out

Purpose

To develop presentations to illustrate something they have learned during this course

Opening Review

Conduct a creative review of the five sessions. You may want to use some of the methods mentioned in "Tips for Leaders" (p. 118).

Say: **We have had five sessions about reaching what we call fringe kids—those who are rejected, bullied, and even the bullies. I believe we have learned a lot and are committed to be more caring about and understanding of the pain of others. Let's take a few minutes to share how these sessions have affected our lives.**

Give kids a quick summary of what they studied in each of the sessions. After describing each session, ask:

• **How did this session impact your thoughts? your attitudes? the way you live?**

Say: **What we have learned can make a powerful difference in our world and is too important to keep in our group. We need to pass on what we have learned.**

Presentation Preparation

Say: **Now we're going to prepare short presentations to pass on what we've learned to others.**

Form groups of four to six. This can be a fun activity and can help build community among people who may not usually associate with each other. Here are some ideas for dividing into groups:

• Put numbers or stickers under chairs and have people find others with the same number or sticker.

138

• Pass out pictures of animals such as cats, birds, goats, monkeys, horses, and elephants. Tell everyone to keep their pictures hidden from others. On "go," have kids begin to make the animal noises. Have kids form groups by locating other kids who are making the same animal noises they are.

After kids have formed their groups, have each group decide which outside group of people it wants to share its presentation with. Here are some suggestions:

• Sunday school classes (either adult or children's)
• other youth groups in your church or in other churches
• church services
• junior church services
• Christian schools
• parent gatherings

Once groups have decided on a target audience, say: **You will have around thirty minutes to plan a five to fifteen minute presentation. The purpose of the outside presentations is to make others aware of fringe kids and how they can help them. You are free to come up with your own ideas, but you can also use any of the activities, stories or other presentation ideas that you've experienced during the past five sessions.**

As you give the following instructions, write them on a flip-chart or newsprint.

Say: **Your group's presentation should include:**
• **an introduction—an explanation of what you're doing and why**
• **one or more key Scriptures**
• **the main part of the presentation—such as a story, an activity, a play, or some other creative presentation**
• **a closing—such as Scripture, a challenge, a song, a poem, or a prayer**

To help kids get started, you might suggest a few presentation ideas, such as:

• Select one of the stories you heard during the sessions. (Be sure you have copies of each to distribute.) Select one or more people in your group to share the story or act it out. Encourage kids to add creativity to their story by using props or other visual aids.

• Read Wanda's letter (p. 88) or the article in Newsweek written by a seventeen-year-old girl (p. 81). Apply them to the sessions you have covered and add Scripture.

• Use the "concentric circle" illustration to explain the meaning of Acts 1:8, describing what it means to go into Jerusalem, Judea, Samaria, and the ends of the earth.

• Present one of the skits in Appendix 3 (p. 149). (Be sure you have copies of each part to distribute.)

Give groups five minutes to decide what to do, then announce that it's time to begin work on the presentation. For those who can't seem to decide, make assignments or give them two or three options to select from.

As groups work on their presentations, go around the room and offer help to any group that's having trouble. Be sure to provide any supplies kids might need for their presentations, such as markers, newsprint, tape, or photocopies of plays or stories you used in the previous five sessions.

Closing

If there is time, have one or more groups give their presentations to the whole class. Over the next week, work with each group to set up a time and place for them to make their presentations to their chosen audience.

Close with prayer. Allow kids the opportunity to pray aloud, asking God to help them find creative ways to reach out to the outcasts in their midst.

APPENDIX 2

assessment tools

To help you determine where you are personally, where your adult leadership is, and where your youth are in terms of creating an embracing Christlike community, we are providing several assessment survey tools. Before you conduct the surveys, read through the following instructions for each item.

YOUTH GROUP CLIMATE SURVEY—
For Adult Leaders

Make copies of the survey, and give a copy to each staff member. Ideally, all members of your youth staff should work on the survey together, coming to a consensus on each item. When in doubt, or when a variety of responses are forthcoming, a rating of 2 (emerging) is probably in order. If it's not possible or advisable to work on the survey together, have each person take the survey individually. Then tally the results.

To follow up on the results, make a list of the statements you rated either 2 or 3. For each item, list the reasons why the group climate scored less than a 1 (successful). Goals to improve the group climate can then be established. It usually works best to set priorities during a leadership retreat or a few consecutive leadership meetings focused on the issue of climate.

After creating a general set of goals, decide which aspects of the climate need to be improved first. Two to three action steps should be agreed upon that can be worked on over two to three months.

If any of the statements 11 through 14 were rated either 2 or 3, they should be addressed first. We suggest that other emerging skills with the highest consensus priority be tackled next.

YOUTH GROUP CLIMATE SURVEY 1—
For Youth

Make copies of the survey and give one to each young person to complete. Collect and then score the results during the following week, creating a tally sheet with numbers 1 through 20. For each survey, tally the frequency of 1s, 2s, and 3s (for statements 1-11) and the frequency of 1s through 4s (for statements 12-20).

Statements for which more than 10 percent of the students picked 3s (statements 1-11) or 4s (statements 12-20) can be considered troublesome, based on past research. If your group's climate is exceptionally good and you want to make it even better, select statements for which 5 percent or more of students selected the least favorable response.

Once the scores are tabulated, at least one youth group meeting should be designated to discussing these issues (1s indicate no problem, 2s moderate problems, and 3s a serious problem).

It can be helpful to keep the scores separate according to gender. Many studies have revealed that girls in our culture often feel harassed in environments where boys joke about or comment too freely on sexual topics. This extends to comments on appearance, which are the most frequent focus of teasing among teens. In addition, issues of sexual harassment in the group are very important to address. To encourage kids to openly discuss these issues, it is important for leaders not to appear to overreact.

We recommend scheduling a meeting in which students can discuss any weaknesses, as well as your group's strengths. Be sure to end the meeting by setting specific goals for improving any areas of weakness.

YOUTH GROUP CLIMATE SURVEY 2—
For Youth

If 10 percent of the group rates the safety statements 17, 18, and 19 with either 3s or 4s, we suggest you examine these issues further. This indicates that some of the young people feel either physically or emotionally unsafe in the group.

Because safety is of utmost importance, we recommend having students complete Youth Group Climate Survey 2 the week after they complete Survey 1. This will help leaders understand why some of the kids feel threatened.

YOUTH GROUP CLIMATE SURVEY
for adult leaders

Rate your group on each statement as either:

(1) Successful

(2) Emerging

(3) Needs improvement

After tallying the results, work together to develop a plan to address each "emerging" item or each one that "needs improvement" based on the information provided in this book. "Emerging" means that the trait, characteristic, or skill is beginning to appear and grow. It implies that, with nurturing, it will become a strength of your youth group.

_____1. The youth group reflects the approximate racial, gender, or ethnic make up of your school or community.

2. Some youth group members could be described as present or former bullies, victims of peer abuse, or bully-victims.

_____ a. Bullies: aggressive reaction pattern

_____ b. Victims: anxious reaction pattern

_____ c. Bully-victims: alternating between anxiety and rage

Note: We suggest that a rating of 1 be assigned when members of these groups *are* represented in the youth group and 3 when they are not.

_____3. A spirit of acceptance pervades the group. Students accept differences in appearance, race, current spiritual understanding, and behavioral style of other people within the group.

_____4. Students actively listen and attend to one another, and relationships are generally characterized by warmth and caring.

_____5. Students attend social activities together, both formal and informal, beyond events sponsored by the youth group.

_____6. Most of the students are able to articulate biblical reasons for extending support to students who hurt or who have been picked on.

_____7. Most of the students are able to articulate biblical reasons for extending support to those who bully others.

_____8. Most students can articulate at least two strategies for intervening safely in a bullying situation.

_____9. Evidence exists that members of the group have either (a) performed a kindness for an individual who has been bullied, or (b) intervened on such a person's behalf.

_____10. Students show a commitment to reaching victims and bullies in their schools.

_____11. Some in the group are behaving inappropriately, such as putting others down, calling others hurtful names, teasing inappropriately, gossiping, or making unkind or inappropriate comments.

_____12. There are definite cliques in the group that are excluding others.

_____13. A few people are dominating the discussions.

_____14. Newcomers are not readily accepted by the group or rarely attend.

YOUTH GROUP CLIMATE SURVEY 1
for youth

On each of the following statements, rate yourself as either:
(1) Successful
(2) Just starting
(3) Need improvement

"Just starting" (2), means that the trait, characteristic, or skill is beginning to appear and grow. With help and growth, it can become a strength in your life or in the group.

Your age_____
Your Sex (circle one)   MALE   FEMALE

_____1. I am comfortable with a wide variety of people from many backgrounds, races, and ethnic groups.
2. I am willing to befriend:
____a. Bullies: kids who often pick on others and seem angry
____b. Victims: young people who get picked on often by others
____c. Bully-victims: young people who sometimes pick on others and who also get picked on often
Note: A score of 1 means you are willing, 3 means you are not.
_____3. I can accept differences in the way various people look and act.
_____4. I have been a friend to at least one victim of bullying.
_____5. It is easy for me to show caring to others.
_____6. In addition to youth group events, I attend other social activities with youth group kids.
_____7. I can give biblical reasons for giving support to students who have been bullied.
_____8. I can think of at least two ways to help someone in a bullying situation.
_____9. I can think of at least two positive ways to deal with infatuations that sometimes happen when I reach out to others. (Infatuations are when a friend believes that more is involved in a relationship than you do. The friend may perceive your kindness as demonstrations of romantic love.)
____10. I have either (a) been kind to someone who has been bullied, or (b) helped such a person.
____11. I am committed to reaching bullies and victims in my school.

For the following statements (12-20), use a different rating scale:

(1) It never, or almost never, happens.

(2) It happens, but not very often (once a month or less).

(3) It happens more than once per month, but less than once per youth group meeting.

(4) It happens very often, at least once a week or more.

_____12. Sometimes when I feel bad or am angry, I call other kids names at youth group.

_____13. I make fun of other kids, but in a friendly, joking way.

_____14. Kids make fun of me at youth group about the way I look.

_____15. Kids make fun of me at youth group about how I act.

_____16. Kids at youth group talk about sex or dating in a way that makes me uncomfortable.

_____17. Kids threaten me at youth group.

_____18. I feel physically unsafe at youth group.

_____19. I feel insecure and emotionally unsafe because of what other kids say or do at youth group.

_____20. Overall, how would you rate the climate (safety and friendliness) of the youth group. Please write a brief statement below about how you see it. Be specific about what you think could improve it.

YOUTH GROUP CLIMATE SURVEY 2

for youth

Rate your youth group on each item as either:

(1) Not true

(2) Often true

(3) Almost always true

Your age_____

Your Sex (circle one)   MALE   FEMALE

_____1. Sometimes the tough kids seem to be in charge of the youth group. This is because the group is not well supervised by the leader(s).

_____2. In our group, there is not a lot of love and caring.

_____3. Small groups (cliques) have formed that exclude others.

_____4. In our group, kids who are unattractive and unpopular feel left out.

_____5. Some kids in the group do not get along well with others. This makes it difficult for the others to include them.

_____6. Some youth come to the group with serious life problems such as physical or sexual abuse, depression, or substance abuse.

_____7. During youth group meetings, a few kids seem to take over discussions at the expense of the others.

_____8. The level of discussion in our group leaves some kids out. Sometimes the words or content are too hard and too complicated.

_____9. In our group, there are very strict "unspoken rules" about what it means to be attractive and acceptable. For example, smaller boys may feel left out. Or girls who are physically unattractive may feel left out.

_____10. Students unsure of their faith feel inferior in our group. That is because those who are more open about faith or more outspoken make them feel that way.

_____11. More popular youth make less popular youth feel unwelcome in our group.

_____12. Name calling, humor, and teasing are often misunderstood by some of our youth.

APPENDIX 3

skits

The following three skits are especially appropriate for Session 4 or Session 6 as one of the presentations. The last skit, *Jesus Went to Samaria*, is for Session 5. Photocopies of the skits may be given to kids before the sessions so they can practice them and put together costumes and props. Or you can distribute them as assignments during a session. Providing simple costumes and props makes them more fun and effective. Be sure to encourage kids to improvise and put the skits into their own words, adding ideas and drama.

SKIT
dabney and daphne

(Dabney is a student with a large zit on his nose. You can place a "zit" on his nose with a red marker or lipstick. Daphne is his classmate.)

DABNEY: *(Enters carrying a backpack or books. He walks into the room where Daphne is sitting.)* Hi, Daphne. Are you ready to study for our algebra exam tomorrow?

DAPHNE: *(Sitting with head in books and writing. Does not look up.)* Yeah, but I'm having a problem with that assignment Mrs. Duddles gave us today. I just can't seem to get it right. It's so confusing. I just hate algebra! Mrs. Duddles doesn't know how to explain it. She spends too much time with the nerds. *(Keeps head down.)*

DABNEY: Calm down, Daphne. I can help you with the assignment. I just finished it in study hall. *(Puts backpack down and sits next to Daphne.)*

DAPHNE: *(Looks up at Dabney.)* Oh, my gosh, Dabney. *(Briefly puts hand over mouth.)* What a zit! *(Laughs and points at it.)* It's huge! The biggest one I've ever seen. Why, it's bad enough to be declared a disaster area. *(Laughs louder.)* Actually, I think you might even qualify for federal aid. *(Laughs even louder.)*

DABNEY: *(Angry)* Well, since you're so amused, see how much fun it is to figure out the assignment by yourself! *(Grabs backpack and storms off.)*

DAPHNE: *(Looks puzzled.)* Now what do you suppose is wrong with him? Can't he take a joke?

SKIT

lavonne and leah

(Lavonne and Leah are talking on the phone, sitting in chairs back to back. Have chairs slightly facing audience so voices project toward them. Provide phones for props or have them use their hands to simulate phones.)

LAVONNE: *(Dials Leah. If possible, have the sound of a phone ringing or someone making the sound.)* Hi, Leah. It's me. Want to hear something really awesome? Danny asked me out. Isn't that great!

LEAH: Congrats, Leah. Tell me all about it. I'm so happy for you!

LAVONNE: Well, you know he's been sitting next to me in youth group for the past month. And, after school today, he finally got the courage to ask me out.

LEAH: So, where are you going? and when?

LAVONNE: This Friday night. We're going to the game, then out for pizza. I'm so excited. He's so cool and funny. You know what he said about you? It was really funny. *(Laughs.)*

LEAH: I can't wait to hear this.

LAVONNE: He said your mom probably named you Leah because she thought you weren't pretty enough to be named Rachel. Isn't that funny? You know, Leah was the ugly sister that Jacob was tricked into marrying. But the pretty one, the one he really wanted, was Rachel. Isn't that funny? *(Laughs louder.)*

LEAH: Oh, yeah. Real funny. I gotta go.

LAVONNE: Wait, let me tell you...Leah. Leah...*(Looks puzzled.)* She hung up on me! Man, is she rude!

SKIT
robbie and randy

(Robbie and Randy are sitting together talking.)

ROBBIE: Hey, that was some practice today.

RANDY: Yeah, I think we're going to win the game Friday.

ROBBIE: You really made some great plays.

RANDY: I feel like I'm on a winning streak now.

ROBBIE: We're all counting on you.

RANDY: You know you can depend on me. But there are some dorks who ought to get off the team.

ROBBIE: Yeah, like Dave and Wayne. They run like they've got lead in their shoes.

RANDY: Or stomachs. *(Laughs.)* They're losers. I don't know how they ever got on the team.

ROBBIE: Yeah. I think they've got brains the size of walnuts. They never get the plays right.

RANDY: I hear they're both failing.

ROBBIE: Good. Then maybe the coach will kick them off the team.

RANDY: And some of the other losers, too.

ROBBIE: Yeah, the coach is too soft. I get sick of him wasting his time on nerds.

RANDY: He's a dork, too.

ROBBIE: Yeah, he's a has-been and a once-was. I think he'd better start practicing this question: "Would you like fries with that?" *(Laughs.)*

RANDY: He looks like he's had a few too many fries himself. *(Laughs.)* He's so out of shape. He's shaped like a pear with a head and legs. *(Laughs.)*

ROBBIE: *(Laughs.)* That's a good one. Well, we better get ready for the youth group tonight. The session is on Unwholesome Talk—whatever that means.

RANDY: Yeah. I hope Dorky Dave and Weirdo Wayne don't show up again. I don't know who invited them.

SKIT

jesus went to samaria

(For this skit, you'll need a Reader, Jesus, James, John, Peter, and a Woman.)

READER: This skit is about a meeting Jesus had with a woman from the country of Samaria. She had a lot going against her.

First, she was looked down on because she was a woman. Back in Jesus' day, most people believed women were not as good as men. Men wouldn't even talk to women in public. They didn't sit together in church. Girls were not even allowed to go to school. All men and boys included this in their prayers: "I thank God that he did not make me a woman."

The Jews looked down on the people of Samaria because they were a mixed race. The Jews said that the people of Samaria did not worship God in the right way or in the right place.

This woman was looked on as a very sinful person because she had been married many times. And now she was living with a man that was not her husband.

(Jesus, James, John, and Peter walk across the stage area. Jesus is in front of them.)

JESUS: I want to go through the country of Samaria.

JOHN: Samaria? What for, Lord? You know we always take the long way around so we don't have to mix with those half-breeds.

PETER: Yeah. We never go through Samaria, even though it would save us many miles and a lot of time.

JESUS: *(Shakes his head.)* You have a lot to learn about God's ways. You call those people half-breeds. Don't you know they are just as important to me as all of you are? *(Jesus walks on ahead of them.)*

JAMES: *(Stops and talks quietly to John and Peter.)* How can he say that? We have pure blood in us. And we worship God the right way. Those half-breeds don't.

JOHN: Yeah, I know. I can't believe God puts up with them at all.

PETER: Me, either. And *I* sure don't want to go through Samaria. I don't want to have anything to do with those people. I hate them—all of them!

JESUS: *(Stops and calls to them.)* Are you coming or not?

(Peter, James, and John look at each other and wait.)

JESUS: Are you men true followers or not? Are you willing to go where I go, like you said you were?

PETER: Uh, yes, Lord. Yes, we are. Come on, guys. *(They frown, look at each other, then walk ahead.)*

JESUS: It's really hot. I think we should rest a while and eat. I'll stay here by this well and get the water. Why don't you three go to town and buy us some food.

PETER: No problem. I'm hungry too. *(They begin to walk off the stage area.)*

JAMES: I sure wish we would have brought our own food.

JOHN: Me, too. No telling what we could catch after eating their food.

(Peter, James, and John exit. Woman comes to the stage area.)

JESUS: Hi. Would you mind getting me a drink of water with your bucket?

WOMAN: *(Looks surprised.)* Oh my goodness! You're a Jewish man. What are you doing talking to me, a woman? And I'm from Samaria!

JESUS: You don't know who you're talking to do you? If you did, you would ask me for a drink of *living* water.

WOMAN: Mister, this well is very deep. Good luck getting any water out of it. You don't even have a bucket.

JESUS: If you drink this water, you'll get thirsty again. But I have a different kind of water. If you drink the water I have, you will never be thirsty again. And that water will become a well of life in you. It will last forever!

WOMAN: *(Sarcastically)* Then please, sir, give me some of *that* water so I'll never be thirsty again.

JESUS: Why don't you go get your husband and then we can all talk together.

WOMAN: *(Looks down.)* Well, uh...well, the truth is, I don't have a husband.

JESUS: You are a very honest person. That's good. I know you have had five husbands. And the man you're living with now is not your husband.

WOMAN: *(Looks surprised.)* What! You know all about me? Why...why...you've got to be from God to know all that. Let's change the topic. What church do you think I should join?

JESUS: That's not what you need to worry about right now. Right now *you* need to get your life in order. You've been looking for love in all the wrong places. I want you to find real love. I want you to find happiness and meaning in your life.

WOMAN: Well, they say the Christ is supposed to come. Maybe when he comes he can tell us what we need to know.

JESUS: Sister, I have good news for you. *I* am the Christ.

(Peter, James, and John walk back to stage area. They look at each other, shake their heads, and whisper to each other.)

WOMAN: Wow! You are the Christ. I'm going back to town and tell everyone! *(Runs off stage area.)*

READER: So this woman, the one looked down on by everyone, became one of the most powerful witnesses for Christ in the Bible. She didn't know a lot, but she told what she knew. She was so excited about Jesus she told everyone she came across, "Come. See a man who told me everything I ever did! He is the Christ!" And because of this woman, nearly the whole town came to believe in Jesus. And, she found that love she had been looking for all her life.[2]

Used with permission to reprint and adapt by Scripture Press Ministries and Dell Coats Erwin. Adapted from the play, "Jesus Went to Samaria" which was formerly published as "Water That Lasts" in the book *Free for Sure: Book 1* (Glen Ellyn, IL: Scripture Press Ministries, 1983), 74-77.

endnotes

Foreword

1. James Garbarino, "Some Kids Are Orchids," Time (December 20, 1999), 51.

2. Jim Hancock, *Raising Adults: Getting Kids Ready for the Real World*, (Colorado Springs, CO: Pinon Press, 1999), 41.

3. Tim Hansel, *Holy Sweat* (Waco, TX: Word Books, 1987), 26.

Chapter 1

1. Excerpted from poetry written by Brian Head, cited in Rita Head, "Remembering Brian," Reclaiming Children and Youth, Vol. 5, Issue 1 (Spring, 1996), 8.

2. Larry Siegel and Joseph Senna, *Juvenile Delinquency: Theory, Practice, and Law*, Seventh Edition (Belmont, CA: Wadsworth/ Thomson Learning, 2000), 376.

3. Richard J. Hazler, John H. Hoover, and Ronald Oliver, "What Kids Say About Bullying," The Executive Educator (November, 1992), 20.

4. John H. Hoover and Ronald Oliver, *The Bullying Prevention Handbook: A Guide for Principals, Teachers, and Counselors* (Bloomington, IN: National Educational Service, 1996), 2.

5. John H. Hoover, Ronald Oliver, and Richard J. Hazler, "Bullying: Perceptions of Adolescent Victims in the Midwestern USA," School Psychology International, Vol 13 (1992), 12.

6. Walt Mueller, "What's so bad about bullies?" youthculture@2000 (fall 1999), 1.

7. Observed from comparison chart presented by John Cloud, "Just a Routine School Shooting," Time (May 31, 1999), 36-37.

8. Reported on National Public Radio in May 1999. Information gathered from Rick Lawrence, editor of Group Magazine, in a personal interview (June 25, 1999).

9. Richard Fransen, "With enough antagonism, violence in schools can happen anywhere—even in Grand Forks," Dakota Student Newspaper, University of North Dakota (April 28, 1999), 4.

Chapter 2

1. William Barclay, *The Daily Study Bible: The Gospel of Luke* Second Edition (Philadelphia: Westminster Press, 1956), 141.

2. Hoover and Oliver, *The Bullying Prevention Handbook: A Guide for Principals, Teachers, and Counselors*, 14.

3. Hoover and Oliver, *The Bullying Prevention Handbook: A Guide for Principals, Teachers, and Counselors*, 15.

4. William Strauss and Neil Howe, *The Fourth Turning: An American Prophecy* (New York: Broadway Books, 1997), 293-295.

Chapter 3

1. "Turning Points: Preparing American Youth for the Twenty-first Century," The Carnegie Council on Adolescent Development, as cited in Patricia Hersch, *A Tribe Apart: A Journey into the Heart of American Adolescence*, (New York: Fawcett Columbine, 1998), 12.

2. Peter L. Benson, "The Troubled Journey: A Portrait of 6th-12th Grade Youth," (Minneapolis: The Search Institute, 1990), 62, 64.

3. James Garbarino, *Lost Boys: Why Our Sons Turn Violent and How We Can Save Them* (New York: The Free Press, 1999), 10.

4. Gleaned from lecture by James Garbarino in Worcester, MA at a symposium entitled "Our Lost Boys: Challenging the Culture of Violence" (Nov. 4, 1999), and from his book, *Lost Boys: Why Our Sons Turn Violent and How We Can Save Them*, 76.

5. Gleaned from an oral interview with Suzanne Jazzman, Clinical Director for the Massachusetts Department of Youth Services (November 5, 1999).

6. Research conducted by Patrick Tolan and cited by James Garbarino in Worcester, MA at a symposium entitled "Our Lost Boys: Challenging the Culture of Violence" (Nov. 4, 1999).

7. Garbarino, *Lost Boys: Why Our Sons Turn Violent and How We Can Save Them*, 163.

8. "The Killer at Thurston High," PBS: Frontline, television show, (January 18, 2000), (www.pbs.org/wgbh/pages/frontline/shows/kinkel/kip/writings.html).

Chapter 4

1. David Grossman, "Trained to Kill," Christianity Today (August 10, 1998), 34.

2. Albert Bandura and Richard H. Walters, *Social Learning and Personality Development* (New York: Holt, Rinehart and Winston, Inc., 1963), 60.

3. Garbarino, *Lost Boys: Why Our Sons Turn Violent and How We Can Save Them*, 23.

4. Deborah Prothrow-Stith and Michaele Weissman, *Deadly Consequences*, (New York: Harper-Collins Publishers, 1991), 14-15.

5. Hersch, *A Tribe Apart: A Journey into the Heart of American Adolescence*, 181.

6. Studies analyzed by psychologist Andrew Weaver, as cited in Garbarino, *Lost Boys: Why Our Sons Turn Violent and How We Can Save Them*, 156-157.

7. Polly Nichols, "Lessons on Lookism," Reclaiming Children and Youth (Summer, 1996), 118-122.

8. John Hoover's research studies of students from midwestern schools confirm this statistic.

9. "Fat-Phobia in the Fijis: TV-Thin Is In," Newsweek (May 31, 1999), 70.

10. Barbara Kantrowitz and Pat Wingert, "The Truth about Tweens," Newsweek (October 18, 1999), 69.

11. Presented by Dr. Jackson Katz in the educational video, *Tough Guise: Violence, Media & the Crisis in Masculinity* (Northampton, MA: Media/Education Foundation, 1999).

12. Hoover and Oliver, *The Bullying Prevention Handbook: A Guide for Principals, Teachers, and Counselors*, 13-14.

13. American Association of University Women and Lewis Harris Associates, *Highlights From Hostile Hallways: The AAUW Survey on Sexual Harassment in America's Schools*, (Annapolis Junction, MD: Eric Document Reproduction Service No. ED 356, 1993), 186.

14. Adrian Nicole LeBlanc, "The Outsiders: How the Picked-on Cope—or Don't," The New York Times Magazine (August 22, 1999), 38.

15. Statistic presented by Dr. Jackson Katz in the educational video, *Tough Guise: Violence, Media & the Crisis in Masculinity*.

16. While Scott Larson holds to this view, he acknowledges that other Christians, such as John Hoover, do not necessarily see homosexual behavior as sin.

17. "News Summary Archive," Religion-Today.com (Wednesday, January 19, 2000).

18. *Current Trends in Child Abuse Reporting and Fatalities: The Results of the 1995 Annual Fifty State Survey*, (National Center on Child Abuse Prevention Research).

19. Statistics presented by Elinor Waskevich, Director of Community Education at the Rape Crisis Center in Worcester, MA, at a symposium entitled "Our Lost Boys: Challenging the Culture of Violence" (Nov. 4, 1999).

20. Survey conducted by the Rhode Island Rape Crisis Center of 1,700 sixth to ninth graders in 1988 by Kikuchi.

21. Study conducted by Levy in 1991 and cited by Emily Rothman, Massachusetts Department of Public Health at a symposium entitled "Our Lost Boys: Challenging the Culture of Violence" (Nov. 4, 1999).

22. Dan Olweus, "Bully/Victim Problems at School: Facts and Effective Intervention," *Reclaiming Children and Youth* (Spring, 1996), 18.

23. Observed from comparison chart presented by Cloud, "Just a Routine School Shooting," Time, 36-37.

24. David G. Fassler and Lynne S. Dumas, *"Help Me, I'm Sad," Recognizing, Treating, and Preventing Childhood and Adolescent Depression* (Middlesex, England: Penguin Books, 1997), 2.

25. Garbarino, *Lost Boys: Why Our Sons Turn Violent and How We Can Save Them*, 41.

Chapter 5

1. Hoover and Oliver, *The Bullying Prevention Handbook: A Guide for Principals, Teachers, and Counselors*, 15.

2. Dietrich Bonhoeffer, *Life Together* (San

Francisco: Harper & Row, 1954), 38.

3. Mother Teresa of Calcutta, edited by José Luis Gonzales-Balado and Janet N. Playfoot, *My Life for the Poor* (San Francisco: Harper & Row, 1985), 15, 18-19.

4. Martin Buber, *I and Thou*, A New Translation with a Prologue and notes by Walter Kaufman (New York: Touchstone, 1970), 28.

Chapter 6

1. LeBlanc, "The Outsiders: How the Picked-on Cope—or Don't," 40.

2. Christopher John Farley and James Willwerth, "Dead Teen Walking," Time (January, 1998), 52.

3. Olweus, "Bully/Victim Problems at School: Facts and Effective Intervention," *Reclaiming Children and Youth*, 20.

4. Hoover and Oliver, *The Bullying Prevention Handbook: A Guide for Principals, Teachers, and Counselors*, 11.

5. Hoover and Oliver, *The Bullying Prevention Handbook: A Guide for Principals, Teachers, and Counselors*, 11.

6. For a more in-depth understanding of this approach, see John Hoover and Glen Olsen's book, *Teasing and Harassment: A Guide for Parents and Teachers: The Frames and Scripts Approach* (Bloomington, IN: National Educational Service, 2000).

7. Andrew Goldstein, "The Victims: Never Again," Time (December 20, 1999), 56-57.

Chapter 7

1. The story of Paul Jensen was written by Larry Brendtro and Scott Larson based on several years of extensive research conducted by Larry Brendtro with the family, court officials, and many others such as neighbors, educators, and foster families who had interfaced with the Jensen family.

2. Some of this material was inspired by a talk given by Mardi Keyes at L'Abri Fellowship called, "Who Invented Adolescence?" (July 15, 1999).

3. Mihaly Csikszentmihalyi and Reed Larson, *Being Adolescent: Conflict and Growth in the Teenage Years* (New York: Basic Books, Inc.,

1984), 71.

4. Mueller, "What's So Bad about Bullies?" youthculture@2000, 9.

5. Kantrowitz and Wingert, "The Truth about Tweens," Newsweek, 71.

6. Grossman, "Trained to Kill," Christianity Today, 38.

7. Grossman, "Trained to Kill," Christianity Today, 38.

8. Walter Bauer, *A Greek-English Lexicon of the New Testament and Other Early Christian Literature*, Second Edition, revised by William F. Arndt and F. Wilbur Gingrich, (Chicago: The University of Chicago Press, 1979), 438.

9. "National Early Teen Survey" conducted in 1998 by KidsPeace, Inc. of Orefield, PA, (1998).

10. Sue Horton, "Mothers, Sons, and the Gangs: When a Gang Becomes Part of the Family," Los Angeles Times Magazine (October 16, 1988), 8.

11. Robert Bly, *Iron John* (Reading, MA: Addison-Wesley, 1990), 93.

12. Linda Nielson, *Adolescence: A Contemporary View*, 3rd Edition (Fort Worth, TX: Harcourt Brace College Publishers, 1996), 309.

13. Scott Larson, *At Risk: Bringing Hope to Hurting Teenagers* (Loveland, CO: Group Publishing, 1999), 38.

14. Nielson, *Adolescence: A Contemporary View*, 3rd Edition, 315.

15. Nielson, *Adolescence: A Contemporary View*, 3rd Edition, 307-308.

16. Mary W. Armsworth and Margot Holaday, "The Effects of Psychological Trauma on Children and Adolescents," *Journal of Counseling and Development*, Vol 72 (Sept/Oct. 1993), 49-56.

17. Statistics given by James Garbarino in Worcester, MA at a symposium entitled "Our Lost Boys: Challenging the Culture of Violence" (Nov. 4, 1999).

18. Nancy Gibbs and Timothy Roche, "The Columbine Tapes," Time (December 20, 1999), 43.

19. Garbarino, *Lost Boys: Why Our Sons Turn Violent and How We Can Save Them*, 117.

Chapter 8

1. Megan Walters, Mexico City, Mexico, "Letter to the Editor," Newsweek (May 24, 1999), 20.
2. James Dobson, *The New Hide or Seek: Building Self-Esteem in Your Child* (Grand Rapids: Fleming H. Revell, 1999), 35.

Chapter 9

1. Shannon Brownlee, "Inside the Teen Brain" U.S. News & World Report (August 9, 1999), 46-47.
2. Steven S. Hall, "The Bully in the Mirror," The New York Times Magazine (August 22, 1999), 35.
3. Henri Nouwen, *Can You Drink the Cup?* (Notre Dame, IN: Ave Maria Press, 1996), 46.
4. Lorraine Adams and Dale Russakoff, "Under scrutiny: Columbine's jock culture," Washington Post, reprinted in the The Boston Globe (June 13, 1999), A26.
5. Tim Dowley, *Eerdmans' Handbook to the History of Christianity* (Grand Rapids, MI: Wm B. Eerdmans Publishing Co., 1985), 87.

Chapter 10

1. Some of these steps are adapted from Josh McDowell and Bob Hostetler, *Josh McDowell's Handbook on Counseling Youth: A Comprehensive Guide for Equipping Youth Workers, Pastors, Teachers, and Parents* (Dallas: Word Publishing, 1996), 163.

Chapter 11

1. John Hoover and Glenn Olsen, *Teasing and Harassment: A Guide for Parents and Teachers: The Frames and Scripts Approach*, Pre-published manuscript copy (Bloomington, IN: National Educational Service, 1999), 10.
2. Garbarino, *Lost Boys: Why Our Sons Turn Violent and How We Can Save Them*, 87-88.
3. Hoover and Oliver, *The Bullying Prevention Handbook: A Guide for Principals, Teachers, and Counselors*, 48.
4. "Risk, Protective Factors, and the Prevalence of Behavioral and Emotional Disorders in Children and Adolescents," *Journal of the American Academy of Child and Adolescent Psychiatry* 28, No. 6 (1989), 262-268.

5. Sharon Beghy, "Why the Young Kill," Newsweek (May 3, 1999), 35.
6. Nancy Gibbs and Timothy Roche, "The Columbine Tapes," Time (December 20, 1999), 43.
7. Wendy Murray Zoba, "Do You Believe in God?" Christianity Today (October 4, 1999), 40.
8. Lynn Vincent, "Gunpoint evangelist," World (October 9, 1999), 18-19.

Appendices

1. James Dobson, *The New Hide or Seek: Building Self-Esteem in Your Child* (Grand Rapids: Fleming H. Revell, 1999), 35.
2. Megan Walters, "Letter to the Editor," Newsweek, 20.
3. Adapted from Dell Coats Erwin, "Water That Lasts," *Free for Sure: Book 1* (Glen Ellyn, IL: Scripture Press Ministries, 1983), 74-77. Used with permission to reprint and adapt by Scripture Press Ministries and Dell Coats Erwin. Adapted from the play, "Jesus Went to Samaria" which was formerly published as "Water That Lasts."

Exciting Resources for Your Youth Ministry

At Risk: Bringing Hope to Hurting Teenagers

Dr. Scott Larson

Discover how to meet the needs of hurting teenagers with these practical suggestions, honest answers, and tools to help you evaluate your existing programs. Plus, you'll get real-life insights about what it takes to include kids others have left behind. If you believe the Gospel is for everyone, this book is for you! Includes a special introduction by Duffy Robbins and a foreword by Dean Borgman.

ISBN 0-7644-2091-7

All-Star Games From All-Star Youth Leaders

The ultimate game book—from the biggest names in youth ministry! All-time no-fail favorites from Wayne Rice, Les Christie, Rich Mullins, Tiger McLuen, Darrell Pearson, Dave Stone, Bart Campolo, Steve Fitzhugh, and 21 others! You get all the games you'll need for any situation. Plus, you get practical advice about how to design your own games and tricks for turning a *good* game into a *great* game!

ISBN 0-7644-2020-8

The Youth Worker's Encyclopedia of Bible-Teaching Ideas

Here are the most comprehensive idea-books available for youth workers. With more than 365 creative ideas in each of these 400-page encyclopedias, there's at least one idea for every book of the Bible. You'll find ideas for retreats and overnighters...learning games...adventures...projects...affirmations... parties... prayers... music...devotions...skits...and more!

Old Testament	ISBN 1-55945-184-X
New Testament	ISBN 1-55945-183-1

Awesome Worship Services for Youth

These 12 complete worship services involve kids in 4 key elements of worship: celebration, reflection, symbolic action, and declaration of God's Truth. Flexible and dynamic services each last about an hour and will bring your group closer to God.

ISBN 0-7644-2057-7
